ISAK DINESEN
Gothic Storyteller

ISAK DINESEN
Gothic Storyteller

Roger Leslie

620 South Elm Street, Suite 223
Greensboro, North Carolina   27406
http://www.morganreynolds.com

ISAK DINESEN: GOTHIC STORYTELLER

Copyright © 2004 by Roger Leslie

Library of Congress Cataloging-in-Publication Data

Leslie, Roger.
  Isak Dinesen : Gothic storyteller / Roger Leslie.— 1st ed.
      v. cm. — (World writers)
Includes bibliographical references and index.
Contents: A restless childhood — A romantic youth — A new life in a
new land — Difficulty and illness — Life in Africa — Making a home —
Leaving Africa — Another new life — Swan song.
  ISBN 1-931798-17-6 (Library binding)
  1. Dinesen, Isak, 1885-1962—Juvenile literature. 2. Women authors,
Danish—20th century—Biography—Juvenile literature. [1. Dinesen, Isak,
1885-1962. 2. Authors, Danish. 3. Women—Biography.] I. Title. II.
Series.
  PT8175.B545Z75515 2004
  839.8'1372—dc22

                         2003022484

Printed in the United States of America
First Edition

World Writers

Isak Dinesen

H.P. Lovecraft

Gwendolyn Brooks

Richard Wright

Henry Wadsworth Longfellow

Nathaniel Hawthorne

Stephen Crane

F. Scott Fitzgerald

Langston Hughes

Washington Irving

Edgar Rice Burroughs

H.G. Wells

Sir Arthur Conan Doyle

Isaac Asimov

Bram Stoker

Mary Shelley

Ida Tarbell

George Orwell

Mary Wollstonecraft

Elizabeth Cary

Marguerite Henry

To Willie and Ima Roberts, with love

Contents

Isak Dinesen at Rungstedlund.
(Courtesy of Rie Nissen.)

Chapter One

A Restless Childhood

There was a popular story often told to young children in Denmark when Karen Dinesen was growing up. The tale goes like this: A man wakes in the middle of a winter night and hears the insistent sound of water dripping. He climbs out of bed and follows the sound of the water outside, where the ground is covered with snow. The night is dark and he has no light. Trying to find the source of the leak, the man stumbles and falls, drags himself up, only to fall again. There are obstacles in his path he cannot see. He does his best to climb over them, all the while searching for the leak. When he finally finds the source, he plugs the leak, then makes his weary way back to bed.

In the morning, the man awakens, steps outside and is surprised and delighted to see that the tracks he made with his erratic stumbling the night before have drawn the outline of a beautiful stork in the snow. Out of difficulty, the man realizes, can come beauty. Because he persevered in his search for the leak, he accomplished something much more impressive than just plugging it up. The obstacles he encountered, the times he slipped and fell down, were all necessary for the creation of the beautiful stork.

Karen Dinesen remembered this story her entire life. She always believed the trials she encountered were her destiny's way of helping her to create something beautiful. Even after losing her father, her husband, her lover, her beloved farm, and her health, she never gave up believing something greater would come of her experiences.

Karen Christentze Dinesen was born on April 17, 1885. She was the second daughter, and her father's favorite. The family lived at Rungstedlund, a rustic and wild former inn with sweeping views of the Baltic Sea located north of Copenhagen. Karen had an older sister, Inger (known as Ea), a younger sister, Ellen (known as Elle), and two younger brothers, Thomas and Anders. Her mother, Ingeborg, had a large family who was very close knit and often came to visit. Karen, called Tanne, knew and loved her many aunts, uncles, and cousins, but it was her father who meant the most to her.

Wilhelm Dinesen was an adventurer, a soldier, a hunter, a politician, and a writer. He was a passionate man who loved new sights and experiences. Before he married, he traveled to North America and lived for a time among a Chippewa tribe, who gave him the name Boganis. When he published his journal from the trip he used the pen name Boganis. He called the book *Letters from the Hunt.* During his visits home to

Wilhelm Dinesen received the cross of the Legion of Honor after serving as a captain in the French army in the Franco-Prussian war of 1870-71. *(Courtesy of N.E. Sinding.)*

Ingeborg Westenholz and Wilhelm Dinesen were married on May 17, 1881. *(Courtesy of N.E. Sinding.)*

Rungstedlund, he regaled his children with stories of his travels. Karen loved and admired her father and wanted to be just like him. She and her younger sister Ellen shared a room. When their father was away, which was often, Karen told stories until the younger girl begged her to stop so she could sleep.

Karen's childhood was full of outdoor adventures and games with her brothers and sisters. She grew into a strong-willed and vibrant young woman. She sometimes suffered from the same dark moods that plagued her father, but when she was happy, Karen was the center of the energy and excitement at Rungstedlund. Then it all suddenly ended.

While Wilhelm Dinesen was attending to his duties as a member of the Danish Parliament in Copenhagen, he hanged himself from the rafters of his room. Modern analysts speculate that a severe bout of depression, perhaps coupled with a diagnosis of the venereal disease syphilis, led to his suicide, but no one knows for certain. He killed himself only a week before Karen's tenth birthday. That afternoon, the family was visiting their grandmother when Karen's Aunt Bess told the children their father was ill. When Karen later asked how he was, her aunt casually replied that he had died. The children were told it was not proper behavior for them to show grief and that they must not speak of their father again.

The family returned to Rungstedlund, accompanied by Aunt Bess, who worked with Ingeborg Dinesen to run the household with strict rules of conduct. The

The courtyard of Rungstedlund, 1891. *(Courtesy of the Royal Library, Copenhagen.)*

children were not allowed in any of the main rooms of the house without an adult's permission, and, once there, could not make any unseemly noise and had to sit perfectly still. They were allowed to do anything they liked in their playroom but could not call upon adults for help. Thomas and Anders were sent away to boarding school. Karen and her sisters remained at home and learned the things deemed necessary to make them good wives: art history, composition, and etiquette. They had very few visitors from outside the family.

Karen resented not being allowed to study the subjects and learn the skills that would make her independent. She thought she had a talent for math, but no one could teach her. Restless and unhappy, she took refuge in her notebook. She began to write down the stories she had been telling, as well as some poetry and several plays that her family performed. Her writing revived happy memories of her father but also reminded her of how trapped and alone she felt at Rungstedlund.

On July 14, 1898, a fire provided Karen her first taste of freedom. One farmhand and many animals were killed in a blaze that damaged or destroyed much of the estate. Ingeborg and the girls were sent to Switzerland to stay while the house was rebuilt. There, Ingeborg enrolled her daughters at the École Benet, an all-girls school. For the first time, Karen learned French and other languages and discovered she had a talent for painting and drawing. She had a taste of life outside of the confines of her family home, and loved it. She did not want to return to Rungstedlund when the house was completed six months later.

Back in Denmark, Karen became a rebellious teenager, much to her family's dismay. When guests came for dinner, she shunned them and sat in the kitchen with the servants—unheard-of behavior in the class-conscious society of the early 1900s. While her sisters sipped tea in the parlor, Karen drank coffee with the maids and other servants of her family's guests.

Many servants shared Karen's flair for storytelling. They amused each other with gossip and ribald tales about luck and destiny. These themes would later inspire the stories that made Karen an internationally famous author.

By the time she was fifteen, Karen was obsessed

The Dinesen children in November 1893: Inger (Ea), Thomas, Ellen (Elle), and Karen (Tanne). *(Courtesy of the Royal Library, Copehagen.)*

with her father. She claimed he had taken over her soul and was living on in her, because only in her could his ideals survive. Her behavior alienated her mother's family even further. They were quick to tease or torment her at any opportunity. Once, Karen confided a secret in her Aunt Lidda, who promptly broadcast it to the entire family over dinner. Karen renounced her mother's family and found refuge in books, reading for hours at a time.

In 1902, Karen announced her intention to enroll at the Royal Academy of Fine Arts in Copenhagen. Initially, her family refused to support her. Karen was insistent, however, and in the end she was given permission to take preparatory art classes at a local school.

Each morning, the coachman drove her to the train station, and each morning Karen celebrated her departure by throwing the lunch they packed her out the coach window. She thought she could achieve a heroic status by self-denial and began to starve herself. She skipped breakfast and lunch and only picked at her dinner. Every hunger pang made her feel more powerful and more in control. Today Karen would probably be diagnosed with anorexia nervosa, but then the disease was not widely known or understood. While Karen eventually returned to eating normally, she would always want to be free from the control of those around her.

Chapter Two

A Romantic Youth

After a year of preparatory classes, Karen was invited to enroll at the prestigious Royal Academy of Fine Arts in November 1903. She left Rungstedlund for Copenhagen, where she would live with a great-aunt, Ellen Plum. Denmark's capital city was an exciting change from home. She took classes at the grand Charlottenborg Palace and, while initially shy, soon enjoyed meeting and socializing with her fellow students. She was elected vice-president of the student union and worked hard.

While studying art, Karen also continued the writing habit she had developed at home. At Christmas 1904, her family performed a play she wrote called *Revenge of Truth*. The plot involves a curse put on the residents of an inn. All the lies they told one night would be revealed as truth in the morning. Full of clever plot twists and eccentric characters, the play reveals Karen's belief in destiny. She saw life "as a kind of marionette

The Dinesen sisters, circa 1903.
(Courtesy of the Royal Library, Copenhagen.)

play in which human beings are the puppets and God is the great puppeteer." Those who tried to betray or deny their destinies would twist and strangle in their puppet strings. Those who surrendered to their fates would find their lives to be works of art.

Karen believed that destiny creates beauty out of struggle. She wrote, "Just when one feels one is floundering in the deepest despair,—'fall into a ditch, get out again,'—is when one is perfecting the work of art of one's life." Her belief that every experience, no matter how painful, was part of the beauty of one's life helped her through many rough times.

She always took great comfort in her short stories. During her time in Copenhagen, Karen wrote many stories under the name Osceola. A tribute to her father's Native American pen name, Osceola was a Seminole warrior who died fighting for his people. His name reflected her conviction that glory only came with sacrifice.

Two of her Osceola stories were published: "The Hermits" appeared in the August 1907 issue of *Tilskueren*, a Copenhagen periodical, and two months later "The Ploughman" was published by another magazine, *Gads danske Magasin*. "The Hermits" tells the story of a young woman trapped in a lonely marriage who finds friendship with the ghost of a sailor. The twist is that the young woman cannot tell whether the ghost is real or a figment of her imagination. "The Ploughman" is a story of redemption: a headstrong but innocent girl discovers a half-man, half-demon, who

Karen Dinesen, about 1907, wearing the dress she bought after selling "The Ploughman." *(Courtesy of the Royal Library, Copenhagen.)*

only she can save from a life of sin. Her third and final Osceola story, "The de Kats Family" was published in 1909. It is a light and lively comedy of manners about a bourgeoisie Danish family.

While Karen worked hard at her writing, her publications met with little critical notice. She enjoyed painting, but was not very successful there, either. At age twenty-three, she dropped out of the Academy, gave up writing, and spent her next few years traveling and being entertained by a group of wealthy friends, including two sets of her distant cousins. Countesses Sophie and Daisy Frijs were sisters, and Barons Bror and Hans von Blixen-Finecke were twin brothers from Sweden. Karen had known these cousins only slightly in her youth.

She had always admired Daisy's wit and elegance and now found her to be someone who could "lift life out of the mundane run and give it poetry." Karen's family did not entirely approve of her association with Daisy, who they considered wild. She was beautiful and attracted scores of suitors. Daisy had much to teach her unsophisticated cousin about flirtation and the opposite sex.

Karen's first experience with love was difficult. She became infatuated with the one man in her social circle who did not return her feelings. Hans Blixen was a handsome, sturdy young soldier. He had an international reputation as the best cavalry rider in Sweden, and, unlike his wild and boorish twin brother, Hans carried himself with the quiet self-assurance of a true aristocrat. In that time and culture, it was not uncommon for distant cousins to fall in love and marry. Karen thought Hans would make a fine husband.

During her adventures with Daisy and their friends, Karen felt keenly the social differences between them. Most of the group came from wealthy, titled families. While the Dinesens were well off, Karen was not as socially secure as her companions. Both Daisy and Hans had titles, which Karen coveted as a sign of true aristocracy. If she married Hans she would then have a title. She enlisted Daisy's help in pursuing Hans.

The two girls tracked Hans around town. When they learned of social gatherings he might attend, they arrived, often uninvited. But Hans was impervious to Karen's charms and the more he ignored her, the more obsessed she became. Karen began to fantasize about marrying him and became convinced her life could never be happy without him.

The situation grew more complicated when Hans's twin brother, Bror, began pursuing Karen. From their birth, Hans seemed to have all the advantages over Bror. He was their father's favorite son. He was more handsome with an accomplished military career and had a large circle of friends. The only thing Hans had not beaten Bror at was finding a wife. For his part, Bror may have fallen in love with the intensity of Karen's passion. It is also possible he decided that Karen was one prize he could steal from Hans before Hans recognized its value. Whether driven by love or jealousy, Bror pursued Karen.

At first, Karen did not object to Bror's attentions.

She did not desire him, but hoped being near him would put her in the same circles as Hans. It was not a wise decision. As they aged the two brothers had less in common, including their friends. Eventually, Bror's attentions began to wear on Karen and she tried to untangle herself from him. But just as relentlessly as she tracked his brother, he tracked her.

In February of 1910, Daisy Frijs married a wealthy man twenty-six years older than she. The wedding was a somber affair. As a bridesmaid, Karen spent time with Daisy before the ceremony and saw her lively cousin depressed at the prospect of life with a man old enough to be her father. Karen was twenty-four, which at that time was considered old for an unmarried woman, and did not have any prospects for a husband or a future. A month after Daisy's wedding, she and her sister fled to Paris.

Arriving in Paris, Karen found herself in a terrible mood, which she described as "a truly horrendous melancholy, the kind in which one hopes both that one will die and kill everyone else at the same time." She was unimpressed by the dazzling sights of Paris, and though she enrolled in art school, she attended classes sporadically. Work did not help her to forget Hans, but she hoped seeing other men might. Karen dated many men in Paris—an American with dandruff-speckled red hair, a nobleman, a pompous German, and a Danish widower with a grown daughter. She became fond of a count named Wedell. When he left Paris, she dealt with his loss by courting a Russian named Raffaelovich.

Raffaelovich was a hurtful reminder of Hans because he would not fall in love with her either.

Karen's whirlwind dating ended when she found an old friend, Eduard Reventlow. A slender twenty-seven-year-old Danish diplomat stationed in Paris, Eduard was engaged to one of Karen's best friends. The Dinesen sisters called upon him soon after they arrived in Paris, and Karen and Eduard renewed an old friendship. The two grew inseparable, spending part of nearly every day together. The more time she spent with Eduard, the happier she became. Karen's sister, Inger, warned her that the romance could lead nowhere, but Karen said she knew and did not care. She was only having fun.

Then Eduard's fiancée, Else, came to visit and Karen's poise was shattered. She sank into depression and could not be consoled. Inger was furious with Karen and scolded her for trying to ruin Eduard and Else's happiness. She insisted the sisters return to Denmark. Karen did not want to go, but she did not know what else to do. Despondent, she followed Inger home. She had been in Paris for only two months.

When the sisters returned to Denmark they found that little had changed. Karen was still in love with Hans, and Bror continued to pursue her. For the next two years, Karen's life went on as it had before she left. She resumed writing, and during this time completed the first of the stories that would eventually be published in *Seven Gothic Tales.*

The stories of *Seven Gothic Tales* are richly detailed and wildly romantic. They are written in the melodramatic style of the nineteenth century and generally center on mysterious, even mystical, experiences that take place among the noble class. The characters recount their stories with grace and acceptance, reflecting Karen's belief that one must not fight one's destiny.

In "The Old Chevalier," a young man is thrown over by the woman he hoped to marry. While mourning her loss, he meets a beautiful woman with whom he falls in love. They spend only a few hours together before she is gone. He then searches for her for years but cannot find her. One day he is visiting an artist who wants to show him a particularly exquisite skull he is sketching from. The man takes the skull into his hand and knows instantly it belongs to the girl he has been looking for. But he never asks the artist for the story of how he came into possession of the skull, sighing only "he would not have known."

Dinesen's belief that all pleasure comes with a price is clearly reflected here. The chevalier's easy acceptance that the woman he longed for is dead reflects his (and Dinesen's) view that her death is the price to be paid for his happiness.

In 1912, Hans Blixen fell in love with and married a wealthy, beautiful, eighteen-year-old debutante. Dinesen was twenty-six, and began seriously considering the idea of marrying Hans's brother. Bror proposed three times before she finally accepted. While the two seemed an unlikely pair from the beginning, Dinesen threw herself into the relationship as passionately as she had pursued his brother. She would later say the early years of her marriage were among the happiest of her life, and was highly critical of people who assumed they could judge a relationship from the outside.

When the couple announced their engagement, Dinesen's family was extremely upset. They liked Bror well enough but considered him a poor prospect for a son-in-law. He was neither intelligent nor refined and preferred hunting and fishing to reading or conversation. Bror did share Dinesen's desire for adventure and excitement. She ignored her family's concerns and the couple began to plan their wedding—and their escape.

In the second half of the nineteenth century, many European individuals and governments turned their attention to the continent of Africa. Germany, England, Belgium, France, Spain, and Italy scrambled to establish territories there—sometimes overpowering local governments by force. England claimed land in Kenya, and cities such as Nairobi became gathering places for wealthy Europeans to meet and conduct business.

England called the lands it claimed its East Africa Protectorate. To solidify that holding, England spent six million pounds to build the Uganda Railroad in 1901. Aristocrats from England and nations friendly to England were encouraged to buy land along the railway route.

Dinesen and Bror each had an uncle who had recently returned from Africa and raved about the place to the young couple. Bror had inherited his family's dairy farm in Denmark, but being a dairy farmer's wife and spending the rest of her life in Denmark did not appeal to Dinesen. Exotic Africa did. She eventually convinced her family to put up money to buy a farm in Africa the newlyweds would manage. The family hoped to see a profitable return on its investment, and Dinesen and Bror hoped to see a new land and new adventures.

Chapter Three

A New Life in a New Land

The Dinesen family invested a sum equivalent to one hundred and sixty thousand dollars (in 1912 money) in an African farm. Bror was sent to oversee the purchase details and to prepare a home. Dinesen would follow him and they would marry there.

From the start, Bror proved himself unreliable. The Dinesens found out, through the mail, that Bror sold the farm they had agreed to purchase in order to buy a much larger coffee plantation. Although neither Bror nor Dinesen knew anything about growing coffee, the land did seem promising and coffee prices were strong. Bror could not have known the soil would be too acidic for the crop. Her family still had misgivings when they saw Karen off on December 2, 1913.

The journey to Africa was very long. Traveling alone, Dinesen first took a ship and then a train to Marseille, France, where she boarded a steamer, sailed though the Red Sea and the Indian Ocean to Mombasa, where she boarded another train for an eighteen hour trip to Nairobi. She spent most of the nineteen sailing days in her cabin, sick and depressed. When she felt well enough to join the other passengers for dinner, their conversations bored her. If these people represented the other settlers she would find in Africa, she was in for a miserable time. The only relief came from Prince Wilhelm of Sweden, who was gallant and charming.

When Dinesen arrived at Aden, a British military port, she was met by a Somali named Farah. He was dressed in a long white waistcoat, called a kanzu, and wearing a formal red turban on his head. Farah was a native of Somalia, a devout Muslim, and was to become one of the closest confidantes she would ever have.

Farah accompanied Dinesen on the final leg of her journey. Bror met them at Mombasa's Kilindini Harbor the next morning. They exchanged wedding vows in a ten-minute ceremony with Prince Wilhelm as their witness and a few hours later boarded a Uganda Railroad train and hosted a small wedding feast in a rattling dining car. There were no sleeping quarters on the train so the couple spent their wedding night in narrow seats as the train chugged toward Nairobi.

Dinesen's romantic view of Africa intensified with her first glimpse of Nairobi and their farm at the foot of the Ngong Hills. Stepping off the train, she inhaled the soft, clear air six thousand feet above sea level. On the drive to their coffee plantation, she marveled at the splashes of natural color. Years later she would describe the landscape: "the sky was rarely more than a pale

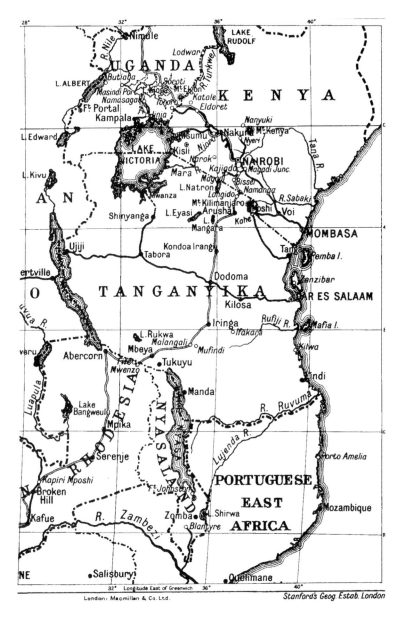

East Africa in 1926.

blue and violet, with a profusion of mighty, weightless, ever-changing clouds towering up and sailing on it." Amid the creepers and liana and lilies growing everywhere, the landscape looked "dry and burnt, like the colours in pottery." To the north, Mount Kenya was "a mosaic of little square maize-fields, banana-groves and grass-land....Towards the West...the brown desert [appeared] irregularly dotted...with crooked dark-green trails."

Fifteen hundred acres of this land belonged to the Baron and Baroness Blixen. When they pulled up to Mbagathi, the first house they owned in Africa, all twelve hundred of their field hands stood waiting for them. They applauded then rushed forward to meet and touch their new mistress. Dinesen's introduction to her new home was overwhelming, but she loved every minute of it.

From the beginning of their life in Africa, Bror was seldom home. An avid hunter, he would go on safari for weeks, even months, at a time. Dinesen was left to attend to the business of running the farm. She began by making improvements to their house. Sweltering heat stagnated in the poorly ventilated rooms, so she designed a veranda to help air circulate better. What began as a small addition became a huge renovation that took more than a year to complete.

In addition to the workmen, the house teemed with people. Farah was Dinesen's majordomo and closest companion. He managed the household staff and farm laborers. His duties included everything from paying

Dinesen with some of her staff outside the house in Africa. Farah is on the bottom right. Dinesen is wearing a necklace he gave her. *(Courtesy of the Royal Library, Copenhagen.)*

all the workers and keeping financial records to chauffeuring Dinesen around the farm and into town. A Somali named Juma oversaw household chores. There was a groom for the stables and a well intentioned but untalented cook named Ismail, or Esa, who ran the kitchen. Throughout the day, groups of *totos*, the young male children of the farm hands, filled the house with noise and laughter while helping in the kitchen or playing with the dogs that roamed the house and yard.

While surrounded by people, Dinesen still had bouts of loneliness. She was discouraged by the language barrier between herself and her staff, and Bror's absence put most of the responsibility for running the farm on her shoulders. She found comfort, as before, in writing. This time she wrote not for herself, but to her family—long, intimate letters all about her life and activities in faraway Africa. These letters helped to mend some of the rifts between Dinesen and her family members, and she grew closer to them than ever before.

With its wooden sidewalks, Nairobi had the rough feel of a frontier town, yet it was an important trade and information center that served as the capital of the British colony in East Africa. When Dinesen looked to the society there for friendships, she was frustrated by still another language barrier. Her English was halting and heavily accented and the aristocratic British women were condescending to her. She did not warm to their snobbish ways and they, in turn, found her eccentric personality and flamboyant style of dress distasteful. Dinesen spent most of her time at home on the farm.

Dinesen in front of Mbogani. *(Courtesy of Thomas Dinesen.)*

There were two major populations of Africans in the region and on the farm: Somalis and Kikuyu. The Somalis were warrior herdsmen who traveled into Kenya from Somaliland and brought with them a deep Muslim faith and a strict code of honor that Dinesen admired. Somalis were generally tall, though Farah was only about Dinesen's height. The Kikuyu were a tribe of self-sufficient Bantu-speaking highland farmers who made up most of the three million indigenous people living in East Africa at that time.

Dinesen set out to learn as much of the languages as

Workers on the farm. *(Courtesy of Thomas Dinesen.)*

she could. Farah took her to visit the families of the farm, serving as an interpreter. She brought pennies and candy for the children and snuff for the old women. She got to know her neighbors and took an interest in their lives. The British women of Nairobi were appalled at her behavior, and Dinesen was further alienated from their society.

Though she knew only basic first aid, Dinesen was able to provide some comfort to the sick and injured. One afternoon, while riding her horse around the farm, she came upon a Kikuyu boy named Kamante whose leg was so infected it was poisoning his entire body. She gathered him up, brought him to her home, and over the next few months slowly nursed him back to health. From then on she was in great demand as a doctor. From nine to ten every morning patients lined up outside her door. With effort and much luck, Dinesen spent her years in Africa treating snakebites, parasites, illnesses, broken bones, burns, and other injuries.

Dinesen announced plans to open a school for her field hands. This shocked the other colonialists even more. She was eager to improve lives through education and wrote home asking for her family to send her a Montessori-trained teacher. That plan never materialized and Dinesen had to settle for a series of missionaries who served as instructors. She converted an old storehouse into a school. The curriculum was exclusively religious because, at the time, the only books translated into Swahili were hymnbooks and the bible. Still, Dinesen believed that some education was better than none.

Because of the school, Dinesen earned a reputation among the farmhands as a leader. She was asked to preside over disputes as a kind of judge, and tried to be fair. Dinesen took her work in Africa seriously and felt great affection for the people she lived with there. Her attitude was unusual for the time and made her the target of scorn and rumor among her European peers. But it made her a respected and loved figure among the people of Africa.

During one of Bror's quick visits home Dinesen contracted malaria. She had violent chills and a high fever. Bror brought her blankets, called a doctor, and then claimed to have business in town. It was Farah who remained at her side for the weeks it took for her to regain strength. Once she recovered, Dinesen resolved to be closer to her husband. She insisted on going with him on the safaris that took him away so often.

In June 1913, the Blixens took a four-day trek through dense bush with three mule wagons and nine servants. Dinesen loved the adventure of sleeping in a tent and taking her turn keeping watch for predatory animals throughout the night. When they reached the Masai Reserve and the savannah where wild animals roamed, she felt the exhilaration of the hunt. On that trip she killed twenty different kind of game, including a lion.

Despite a plague of flies and the constant threat of attacks by wild animals, Dinesen declared "there is nothing in the world to equal" going on safari. She was free of the responsibilities of the farm and spent the day stalking prey or exploring the rugged and beautiful land. In the cool of the evening, she would bathe in a nearby river while servants prepared dinner. After eat-

Bror and Karen on safari in 1914, with two lions they shot. *(Courtesy of the Royal Library, Copenhagen.)*

ing, the group would settle around the fire to drink wine and tell stories long into the night. It was easy for Dinesen to see how Bror preferred safaris to the mundane routines of home. She was happy on the trip and enjoyed the time with her husband. But a year later, their idyllic lives were interrupted by war.

The outbreak of World War I was triggered by the assassination of Archduke Francis Ferdinand of Austria-Hungary in June 1914. On August 5, England declared war on Germany. Three days later, British warships off the coast of East Africa attacked a German settlement to the south. Because he was Scandinavian, Bror feared he might be taken for a German sympathizer. To avoid trouble, he immediately volunteered as a non-combat intelligence officer for Britain's Lord Delamere. His job took him to the German border, far from Dinesen and the farm.

Dinesen joined the war effort by taking charge of a railway camp where border runners brought news for her to telegraph to headquarters in Nairobi. One day word came that an internment camp was being set up to offer protective custody to all the white women of the region. Dinesen was determined not to spend the war hiding while the men enjoyed all the danger. She kept to her post. Bror sent word he needed a wagon train of supplies, and asked his wife to find a skilled man to drive it. When the man she found was arrested, Dinesen decided to take the supplies herself.

There were two wagons so heavily loaded each required sixteen oxen to pull them. Dinesen took twenty-

Dinesen outside her tent while on safari, 1914. *(Courtesy of the Royal Library, Copenhagen.)*

one Kikuyu, a gun-bearer, her old cook, and Farah with her on the trip. They drove nine more oxen alongside the wagons. Dinesen spent three months making forays like this one to Bror's station from headquarters, ferrying supplies along dusty, rutted roads through wild territory. Lions often attacked the oxen, especially at night. The threat of enemy soldiers was constantly on the horizon. Dinesen could not have been happier.

Chapter Four

Difficulty and Illness

As the war escalated, soldiers replaced civilians at their volunteer posts. Military authorities released Dinesen from her railway position and sent her back to the farm. In November of 1914, the German army pummeled British troops in Africa and made off with their supplies. The British turned against the Africans, accusing them of not supporting the war. The Africans accused the British of being incompetent. The settlers were divided between support for their countries of origin and support for the country that protected their lands. Morale in Africa sunk so low that 1915 became known as the black year.

The farm faced a shortage of workers as the field hands were impressed into the army. A fever swept through the oxen and killed almost all of them. Then Dinesen became seriously ill.

At first, Dinesen thought she was suffering from a reoccurrence of malaria. She lost weight, felt feverish, had little strength, and barely slept. To help her sleep, she began relying on larger doses of a powdered drug called Veronal. One night, either accidentally or on purpose, Dinesen took a nearly fatal overdose. Bror happened to pass through the bedroom and found her unconscious on the floor. He managed to revive her, and she spent the next two days vomiting. A trip to a doctor in Nairobi revealed her symptoms were not of malaria but of the venereal disease syphilis.

Bror's frequent absences from the farm were always explained as safari trips. Sometimes when Dinesen was in Nairobi for supplies, she overheard gossip that implied Bror was having affairs. She had always ignored the rumors because they came from the same women who ostracized her for her liberal politics. Now Dinesen learned the truth: Bror had consistently been unfaithful. He had an affair with the wife of a good friend of theirs, a man who had lent them money, and he had affairs with some of the local women—including one from a tribe that was devastated by a syphilis epidemic.

Bror never suffered any outward symptoms of the disease, but he did pass it on to his wife. The doctor in Nairobi said Karen's was one of the worst cases he had ever seen. Because she waited so long to seek help, Dinesen was already experiencing the secondary stage. The doctor urged her to leave Africa immediately to get treatment in Europe. In a deep depression, another effect of the disease, Dinesen refused to go.

The doctor prescribed Dinesen mercury pills to alleviate some of her symptoms. Commonly prescribed for

Dinesen on safari. *(Courtesy of the Royal Library, Copenhagen.)*

illness and depression, mercury pills had the unfortunate side effect of being poisonous. Mercury is no longer used as medicine today, and even old-fashioned mercury thermometers are being replaced by safer, non-toxic alternatives. Dinesen would take mercury for a year before the metal poisoned her system, resulting in neurological damage.

As for Bror, she said "there are two things you can do in such a situation: shoot the man, or accept it." She decided to accept his infidelities and they reconciled on a two-month safari trip. When they returned, Dinesen was sicker than ever and finally agreed to leave Africa for treatment.

Securing passage to and from Africa in the midst of a war was difficult, but Dinesen managed to get to Paris in April of 1915. Venereal disease specialists there could not guarantee she would ever be cured. Her only hope was to undergo long, painful treatments that were impossible in war-torn France. She saw no choice but to return to Denmark.

Dinesen wrote to her mother that she was suffering from a rare tropical disease. She arranged to be treated in the general ward of the hospital, not the ward for venereal diseases. She spent three months in the hospital in Copenhagen. Here treatment there included taking an arsenic-based medication called Salvarsan that was so strong it could be toxic. The arsenic temporarily poisoned her system, causing pounding earaches and headaches, stomach cramps, and burning in her hands and feet. She believed the treatments were killing her. If they did not, she thought her loneliness might.

The disease pained Dinesen almost as much as being away from Africa. While in the hospital, she wrote a poem called "Ex Africa" which eloquently expresses her longing to return to the place where she had been so happy. Bedridden in Denmark, she dreamed of returning to the only place where she felt free.

After her release from the hospital, Dinesen remained in Denmark for nearly a year. She returned to Rungstedlund where her mother attended to her. Dinesen eventually confessed to her mother the truth about her illness and was grateful her mother accepted the news quietly and without passing judgment. Dinesen was home to see both of her sisters marry, and to help her brother convince their mother to let him enlist in the Canadian Army. Thomas shared the sentiments of his father and sister, that there were times when it seemed necessary to offer one's life for a cause. In the summer of 1916, Bror came to Denmark with encouraging news. Initially, the war had devastated their farm. But it had also pushed coffee prices sky-high. They should be able to make high profits from their crop. Because their original investment had become profitable, the Dinesen family incorporated the Karen Coffee Company and sold shares to family and friends. They raised a good deal of money and the Blixens made plans to return home. On January 26, 1917, they were back at the farm.

The Karen Coffee Company had a terrible first year. Coffee prices were still high, but their crop was ruined by drought. The Blixens found themselves penniless.

After leaving Denmark in triumph, Karen had to write home to ask for more money.

Despite their financial trouble, the Blixens moved into a new home a little closer to Nairobi. As their first house had been, this one was made of gray fieldstone and was built in a forest of tall trees that helped to block the scorching African sun. The rooms had high ceilings, large windows, and were breezy and cool. The house still contained the fully stocked library of its previous owner: Dinesen felt as though she had returned to paradise. The Africans called the house *Mbogani*.

1917 was a year of bad news. First, the coffee crop failed. In March Karen learned that Bror's brother Hans had died in a plane crash. Dinesen had put her infatuation with Hans behind her but his death was still a shock. Just a few months later, a letter from Paris reported that Daisy Frijs, their cousin and Karen's best friend in Denmark, had committed suicide. Dinesen was devastated. She remembered Daisy as wild and lively. It was hard to reconcile that image with one of a woman who would take her own life. Daisy had been unhappy in her marriage and Dinesen wondered if that contributed to her final act.

It was an emotional time, and Dinesen relieved her feelings in her letters. She wrote extensively to her brother Thomas, fighting in France, and to her mother in Denmark. The mail was nearly three months behind so letters served not just to communicate news—which would surely be old by the time anyone read it—but to

Bror and Dinesen in the drawing room of their African home. *(Courtesy of the Royal Library, Copenhagen.)*

offer some peace to the writer. Dinesen wrote little fiction during this time, but comforted herself with letters and painting. Alone again, she found solace in capturing on paper the soothing lines and rich colors of her surroundings.

In 1918, Farah chose a wife and, while he remained a loyal servant, spent much less time with Dinesen. As a wedding gift, she had a small house built for the couple. Dinesen was happy for him, but missed his comfort and support. When the Blixens were invited on a buffalo hunt, she relished the opportunity to take a break from the farm.

The Blixens had befriended a cattle rancher, Frank Greswolde-Williams, who had lived in Africa for many years. He was one of several people they spent time with in early 1918 who would later serve as models for characters in Dinesen's stories. She was very happy in this group, which was made up of tough but cultured hunters and soldiers. There was much laughter and little pretension.

One member of the group was a man named Erik Otter, who was legendary for choosing to live with black soldiers over white during his military service. He was very close to the Africans, and Dinesen admired him for that. He was an exceptional soldier, had earned many accolades on the battlefield, but was not pompous or vain. He studied Islam and taught Dinesen much about the religion. She became greatly enamored of him, then infatuated, and they began having an affair. Otter took Dinesen on safari with him, one of her great pleasures.

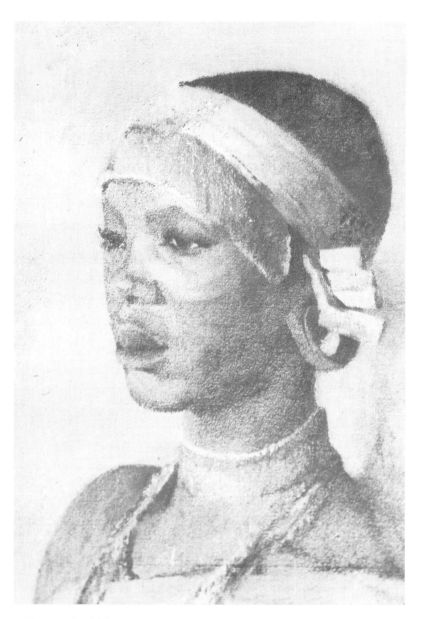

Dinesen painted this portrait of a young Kikuyu woman in the 1920s. *(Courtesy of the Royal Library, Copenhagen.)*

In the end, however, Otter's personality was too serious to hold her affection. He asked her repeatedly to divorce Bror and marry him, but Dinesen always refused. Her feelings for Bror were only comradely, she knew she did not love him and their marriage would not last, but Otter did not have the spark of humor she sought in a companion. She returned to her husband.

Chapter Five

Life in Africa

The summer of 1918 brought another drought and the coffee crop failed again. Food became scarcer for people and animals. In Denmark, the Dinesen family grew restless at two straight years of losses from their African investment. They wrote Karen long letters accusing Bror of mismanagement. She defended her husband and insisted things would get better, even offering to buy back shares in the farm—something which she could not afford to do.

Despite Dinesen's outward confidence, inwardly, she harbored her own doubts. The farm was in trouble, and she had suffered a series of personal losses—beginning with the deaths of Hans and Daisy—that left her shaken and sad. The next major loss was of her beloved deerhound, Dusk. Dusk had been a wedding present to Dinesen and she had brought him to Africa. He was a large, handsome dog and she was extremely fond of him. Dinesen took Dusk with her everywhere she could.

In August 1918, on the way to pick up Bror in Nakuru, Dinesen stopped at a train crossing. Dusk was nosing around on the tracks when she looked up to see a train coming toward him. Dinesen ran to the dog and, at the last second, pulled him off the tracks. The train just grazed them, knocking them out of its path to safety.

The next day, Dinesen was with Bror and their book-keeper, Huth, when the car broke down. Bror took his wife to town on a motorcycle and left Huth to wait with the car for help. Dusk could not come on the motor-cycle, so Dinesen left him behind. She begged Huth to be careful with Dusk and to keep him on his leash. "You *must* take good care of him," she demanded. "I risked my life for him yesterday and would so again today; I prize him more than anything in this world."

Huth eventually returned to the farm, but without Dusk. He explained that he had taken Dusk hunting and the dog had run off. Dinesen and Farah immediately boarded a train back to Nakuru; she worried the entire fifteen-hour ride.

In town, some Somalis told Dinesen they had seen Dusk. He had slept at their camp one night and then disappeared in the morning. For three days, Dinesen searched for her dog, offering a large reward for any information about his whereabouts. Farah finally found him in the mountains, weakened, injured, and dying from a fight with a zebra he had killed. The dog wagged his tail for Farah, but could not take any water or food. He died a few hours later. Dusk was too large to carry back to town so Farah buried him on a hillside.

Dinesen with some of her Scotch deerhounds. *(Courtesy of the Royal Library, Copenhagen.)*

Dinesen was devastated. "If I live to be seventy," she said, "I believe I will never think of him without weeping." She took comfort in believing that when she died, she would see Dusk again and "most fervently beg his forgiveness for leaving him."

A few weeks later, Dinesen herself was badly injured falling off of a mule. She tore her leg open on a rock and the wound became infected. She had to be taken by oxcart to the Nairobi hospital, where a doctor performed an operation that saved her leg but left her with a terrible scar from hip to knee. She was bedridden, again, for several weeks. Bror came and went from the farm but no longer gave her excuses for his absences—they both knew where he really was.

Divorce was not unheard of in the 1920s, nor was it particularly frowned upon, but Dinesen never asked Bror for a divorce, despite his constant womanizing. Having the title of Baroness was important to her. She was not willing to give it up. Bror had passed on to her a debilitating disease that required trips to Europe for painful and embarrassing treatments, but he made few demands upon her and enabled her to live and work on the farm. The Blixens came to an arrangement: neither would question the other's affairs, and they would co-exist peacefully at home.

In 1920, Dinesen had to make another trip to Denmark. She spent five months in the hospital. Bror accompanied her but soon returned to Africa. While she was at home, Dinesen still hid the truth about her illness from her family, but finally confessed—or at least hinted about—Bror's infidelities. Her family was angry. They had not liked him from the beginning and now wanted him out of their family and out of their business. The Dinesens pressured Karen to ask for a divorce and spoke of removing Bror as farm manager. Karen regretted having said anything because it gave her family license to intrude into her life. She hurried back to Africa as soon as she was able.

The couple was already in financial trouble because of two years of poor crops but Bror did little to manage the farm while Karen was gone. She returned to a home so badly neglected she barely recognized it. High weeds covered the grounds and the coffee bushes were withering. Not only was the house in shambles, but Bror had also incurred huge debts for the purchase of clothing, furniture, hotel rooms, and bar tabs.

As Dinesen set to work cleaning up she learned Bror was having an affair with a married woman from their circle, Cockie Birkbeck. It was not the infidelity that troubled her as much as it was that the openness of it reflected badly on them. Bror did not give up Cockie when his wife had returned. Dinesen decided she had finally had enough. She told him to leave the farm until he could demonstrate some responsibility toward his debts and their business. Still, she did not ask for a divorce—all she wanted was for him to be more responsible. Bror left without argument.

Dinesen threw herself into rebuilding the farm. There was a great deal to be done and she was always happiest when she felt needed and important. Africa offered her many opportunities to feel as if what she was doing was worthwhile, much more than living an upper-class life in Denmark. During her time in Africa she was absorbing the sights, sounds, people, and events that would become the backbone of her great work, *Out of Africa*. Part memoir, part novel, *Out of Africa* is a love story about a woman and a place.

In May of 1922, Dinesen spent three weeks in a nursing home in Kenya. The mercury pills and arsenic she had taken during the syphilis treatments had wrecked her body. She would be in pain for the rest of her life. While in the nursing home, she had a recurring dream that something terrible happened to her older sister, Inger. She believed in dreams and premonitions and worried that her fears would be realized. She was right: a telegram came announcing that Inger had died while giving birth to a stillborn child.

Dinesen returned to the farm, grieving from the news of her sister's death, to find that more trouble awaited her. She had made it a rule that no children were allowed to ride on the back of the oxcarts that moved goods around the farm. But the children disobeyed, and a little girl named Wamboi was killed when the basket she was carrying snagged on the wagon frame and pulled her under its heavy wheels. The police could not decide who was to blame for her death. Wamboi's tribe was superstitious about touching corpses, so her body lay in the street for three days before Dinesen buried the girl herself.

Africa was a romantic place to Dinesen, but she saw

much hardship and many terrible things. The Blixen's cook was poisoned by his own wife, and, despite strong evidence against the woman, the police refused to bring charges. A seven-year-old boy named Kabero got hold of a gun. He and some friends were clowning around when Kabero pointed the gun at them and, not knowing it was loaded, pulled the trigger.

Alone at her house, Dinesen heard the gun go off. Moments later, a man came to the house calling for help. She and Farah gathered dressings and disinfectant and ran to the little house where the boys had been playing. In the kitchen, gunpowder still floated in the air. The gun lay on a table beside a hurricane lamp. The boy who shot it had fled and would never be seen again.

A boy named Wamai lay unconscious, moaning on the floor. His friend Wanyangerri sat forward, shrieking, as blood gushed from his face where his jaw had been shot off. Dinesen slipped on blood as she ran to him. Farah held the boy's head still as she wrapped it tightly to try to stop the bleeding. Wamai was still unconscious. Farah went for the car and they rushed the boys to the Native Hospital in Nairobi.

Wamai stirred as they pulled him from the car onto a stretcher. Wanyangerri was still screaming and clung tightly to Dinesen. A doctor gave him a sedative then assessed the situation. Wamai was dead. Wanyangerri would live, but was severely disfigured.

The strain of these tragedies, the separation from Bror, and worry about the farm wore her down. The arrival of Inger's widower, Viggo de Neergaard, added to the stress. Still grieving over the loss of his wife and child, de Neergaard came to the farm to escape Denmark and to throw himself into work. Dinesen gave him Bror's managerial duties, which was a help to both of them, but found his presence a sad reminder of her sister's death.

A visit from her brother Thomas lifted her spirits. He arrived a true war hero, having been awarded the Victoria Cross, Britain's highest medal for valor, fighting in France. Like many of the men she admired, Thomas was unruffled by hardship and excited to experience life in Africa. Dinesen was eager to show off her world. They spent hours sharing stories of their adventures. Bror had all but officially moved out, so Thomas was her only real companion. He stayed for two years.

It was Thomas who finally told Dinesen the truth about her father's death. They were reminiscing about him, and Dinesen was happy to find that Thomas admired him as much as she did. She was surprised that Thomas knew so much about him—he was only six when Wilhelm died. Her brother reported that he had questioned relatives over the years and learned more about their father. He then, straightforwardly, told his sister the truth: Wilhelm had died by his own hand. It might have been to avoid the disgrace of suffering from syphilis, Thomas said.

The news was shattering—yet it gave Dinesen some comfort. She had always believed she and her father had a special connection. For a while, as a young girl, she had even believed her father inhabited her soul.

Thomas Dinesen during World War I. *(Courtesy of the Royal Library, Copenhagen.)*

The fact that he might have borne the same disease that so devastated her was an irony Dinesen could appreciate. She was grateful to her brother for telling her the truth.

One of the projects Thomas undertook was to build a factory for processing coffee. He threw himself into the project, drawing up plans and supervising the construction. The completed building made him very proud: it sheltered important equipment and made the coffee production more efficient. Thomas soon learned, however, that in Africa few man-made things last forever.

A few months later, Dinesen was awakened by her servant Kamante. "Msabu," he said, "I think you had better get up. I think that God is coming."

When Kamante had said those exact words once before, he had been referring to a massive grassfire burning across the hills. This time, Dinesen looked out the window to see flames consuming Thomas's factory. The entire farm was awakened to bring water from the pond, but it was too late. The building was completely destroyed, along with all the equipment inside.

The fire was just another setback to Dinesen, but her brother took it hard. He saw the farm as a constant struggle to survive against the odds. Toward the end of his stay, their uncle, Aage Westenholz, came to visit. He brought the news that the family wanted to rid itself of the farm. He had been the driving force behind the family's initial investment and now was the driving force behind the decision to sell. The farm, he had decided, was too risky. It was time to cut their losses.

Thomas put aside his own misgivings and joined Karen to defend the farm to Westenholz. The three argued for days about what to do. Dinesen was adamant that the farm could be saved and, finally, Westenholz offered to keep the investment if his niece would agree to new conditions. Dinesen saw no other choice, though she was furious at her family's interference and lack of confidence.

The relationships she had only recently mended were soon stretched thin again. Dinesen even quarreled with her mother, the one family member she had managed to get along with for so many years. She wrote to her mother that she and Bror were separated, but asked Ingeborg to keep this news in strictest confidence. In an echo of the betrayal of her childhood, Ingeborg shared her daughter's story at a family gathering. Dinesen was soon deluged with letters urging her to divorce her husband. She was furious and threatened to cut off all communication. She needed support, she told her mother, not criticism or advice. Ingeborg made up with her daughter and their correspondence continued.

Thomas left Africa and, once again, Dinesen found herself alone. It was Denys Finch Hatton she looked to for company now.

Chapter Six

Making a Home

Karen Dinesen first met Denys Finch Hatton in April 1918 at a dinner party. They met again a month later and by the end of the second visit she knew she was passionately in love. She called Hatton her "ideal." He was a sensuously handsome man, cultivated and intelligent, with a wicked sense of humor and a fondness for the absurd. Hatton was as comfortable on the plains of Africa as he was in the opera box. He was easy-going but shrewd, and seemed to be always on the move. Soon after he and Dinesen met, he began to use her house as a home base between adventures. He would be there for a week or two before leaving again for months at a time. While Thomas was at Mbogani, Hatton came to visit only when her brother was absent.

Wildly happy when he was with her, depressed when he was not, Dinesen fell into the old habit, as she had with her father and Hans, of pinning all her happiness on another human being. She was relieved to discover

Hatton was not a womanizer like Bror, but he was almost as hard to keep.

Schooled in Greek and Latin at Eton College and Oxford, Hatton was articulate and intelligent with a knack for remembering brief lines and even long passages from literature. His conversations with Dinesen were peppered with references to great books, quotations from Shakespeare, and lines of poetry. With other people he was more reserved, unwilling to appear snobbish, but her cultured background gave him the freedom to talk of art and literature.

Once Bror moved out, Hatton and his best friend, Berkeley Cole, all but moved in. They stocked the house with fine tobacco and taught Dinesen to be a wine connoisseur. They loved to surround themselves with beauty and convinced her always to use her finest Danish china and glassware whenever they came to dinner. When one, or both, of the men were in residence, Mbogani was a happy place. But when they were absent, Dinesen felt more alone than ever.

As the relationship between Dinesen and Hatton deepened, the pattern of his visits remained the same. She was frustrated by how self-centered he was. He arrived unannounced, stayed for as long as he wanted, and then left without saying where he was going or when he would return. Still, she could not help but be happy to see him.

Part of Hatton's charm was his ability to remain cool in the face of danger. One night, the couple was in the living room after dinner when the farm manager came running into the house. He reported that two lions had broken into the oxen's shed. He had run the lions off but not before they had killed two of the farm's strongest oxen. Dinesen feared her horses would be next. The farm manager wanted permission to put poisoned meat out for the lions, but Dinesen and Hatton decided to go after the animals themselves.

It was a dangerous proposition. Shooting at night was extremely difficult and, if they missed, the lions might very well attack. But moments such as this were exactly what Dinesen longed for. She turned to Hatton and said, "Let us go and risk our lives unnecessarily." Then she added in Danish, "He lives free who can face death."

Hatton carried the gun while Dinesen held a battery-powered lantern. They dragged one of the dead oxen out into a clearing and waited, knowing the lions were likely to return to feed on their kill. Out in the darkness there was a roar. They waited, then the noise came again, closer. At Hatton's command, Dinesen held the lantern over his shoulder and flicked the light on. There was a lion, directly in front of them. Hatton shot and the lion fell.

Hatton yelled for her to move the lantern light. Dinesen swung it around to find the other lion behind a coffee bush. Hatton shot again and the second lion went down.

The noise of the gunshots brought farmhands running to marvel at their bravery and skill. They began to call Dinesen "the Lioness" or, instead of Baroness von

Denys Finch Hatton.
(Courtesy of the Royal Library, Copenhagen.)

Blixen, Lioness von Blixen. It was a title that meant much to her and she would wear it proudly for the rest of her life.

The outdoor adventures of Hatton and Dinesen were balanced by quiet and happy times at home. When Hatton arrived, she made sure his favorite meals were prepared. If she were out riding, he would open all the doors and windows of the house and play music on the gramophone he had brought her so that, as she neared the house, Stravinsky or Beethoven greeted her. They always dressed formally for dinner, talking about art or literature well into the night. Propping pillows in front of the fireplace Hatton would play the guitar or Dinesen would tell stories.

While Dinesen did not write much fiction during this time, she was always gathering and polishing material. Writing letters to her family and friends was one way she practiced her story-telling skills—another was listening to the story-tellers around her, and yet another was the challenge of entertaining Hatton. The more he enjoyed his time at Mbogani, the longer he would stay. Dinesen used her stories like ropes to try to hold the restless man close.

Her true depth of feeling for Hatton shows in her letters. Writing to her brother Thomas, Dinesen called Hatton "the joy of my life." Later, she wrote simply, "I believe that for all time and eternity I am bound to Denys, to love the ground he walks upon, to be happy beyond words when he is here, and to suffer worse than death many times when he leaves." She could communicate these emotions to her family, but she would not dare to tell them to Hatton. He insisted that they would never marry.

In 1922, Bror asked Dinesen for a divorce. He wanted to marry his long-time mistress, Cockie Birkbeck. Dinesen was upset at the prospect of losing her title. She had lost her husband a long time ago. She put off his divorce petition as long as she could, then finally agreed. They would divorce, as amicably and quickly as possible. Bror would marry Birkbeck, and remain affectionate towards his ex-wife for as long as he lived.

The divorce did not have any impact on Dinesen's relationship with Hatton. During the legal proceedings she wrote a lengthy essay called "Modern Marriage and Other Considerations" outlining her view that love and marriage are two separate things. It was Dinesen's contention that too many people believed love should lead to marriage. She argued that a marriage should be based on a mutual commitment to a goal. Love, she wrote, did not bind two people together. She was writing from experience. She and Bror had cared for each other, but their different desires in life had ruined their marriage. She and Hatton were very much in love, but marriage might have ruined their affection.

After her divorce was finalized, Dinesen experienced another bout of depression. She was in pain from syphilis, and alone on a farm that could be sold out from under her at any moment. Her family in Denmark was unhappy with their investment and she was constantly writing to them, begging for more time. At times such as this, her responsibilities felt overwhelming.

Her mood changed when she realized she was pregnant. While married to Bror, she had wanted to conceive but assumed syphilis had made her sterile. Now she was thrilled to discover she was carrying Hatton's child. It was scandalous for an unmarried woman to have a baby and her financial situation was precarious, but Dinesen was thirty-seven years old and delighted to be pregnant. But only a month later she miscarried. She was devastated; Hatton never knew she was pregnant.

Several years later, Dinesen became pregnant again. She miscarried for a second time, but not before she informed Hatton about his child. It is rumored that Hatton suggested she abort their baby, then backed down when Dinesen refused. He did make it clear that having the baby would be her choice—Dinesen would raise the child alone, as she did almost everything else.

Though she never had a child of her own, there were always children around the house. Dinesen loved them all very much, especially a boy named Kamante, the child whose infected leg she had doctored soon after arriving in Africa. He was a charming but odd character who Dinesen found utterly compelling. When the cook was poisoned, Kamante came to help out in the kitchen. She sent him to study with the best chefs in the region and found him to be a great comfort to her.

While driving to town and back one day, Dinesen twice passed a group of children who had captured a tiny fawn and were trying to sell it on the side of the road. Distracted by business concerns, she ignored the scene. It was not until she had gone to bed that she realized the animal's life was in danger. Racked by guilt for not doing anything sooner, Dinesen roused her entire staff and sent them out into the night to find the fawn and bring it home.

The next morning, Farah appeared with the tiny creature and Kamante was given the job of feeding it with a bottle. Bushbucks are small, shy, and solitary African antelope that live on grasses and other vegetation. The infant bushbuck Dinesen called Lulu would grow to stand about two feet high at the shoulder and weigh about one hundred pounds. She became a favored pet around the house, trailing after her mistress and tormenting the dogs, despite her small size, with demands for their preferred sleeping spots. Dinesen writes about her with great emotion in *Out of Africa*, remembering fondly her queenly behavior and elegant manners. Lulu eventually left Mbogani to return to the brush, but for years she would return to the door of the kitchen and Dinesen always looked forward to seeing her again.

Life in Africa was sometimes beautiful, sometimes dangerous, but never dull. Dinesen felt a strong connection to the people she lived among and often took their side in conflicts with Europeans. Dinesen became known for her politically pro-native stance—one that was not popular at the time.

White Europeans usually viewed Africa as a literal and figurative goldmine. The enormous continent was rich in resources and game. Whites who moved there thought of themselves as settlers and claimed as much

Dinesen feeding Lulu, the infant bushbuck she rescued, from a bottle. Animals were an important ingredient in Dinesen's happiness. *(Courtesy of the Royal Library, Copenhagen.)*

land as they liked, ignoring the protests of the people who lived on it already. Europeans generally saw native Africans as an inferior race, less civilized and culturally developed. The two cultures were different in almost every way, from customs to language to dress to technology. These differences reinforced European notions of superiority.

By the time Dinesen came to Africa, Europeans had been relying on African labor to run their farms for many years. Some workers were paid, some were given food and housing, some got very little recompense at all. Diseases whites brought with them took a tragic toll on the native population. After the war there was a severe shortage of farm labor. Many white Europeans petitioned the government to force natives to work on their farms and on highway and railroad improvement projects. Dinesen was one of the very few who were opposed to this policy of forced work.

Dinesen was not active enough in politics for her views to cause her any real trouble, or to have much impact. However, her belief that native Africans deserved voting rights and a chance to work their own land was akin to treason as far as her contemporaries were concerned. The school she built for her workers, the medical care she provided, and the respect she gave them were unusual and unpopular among the Europeans, who whispered that these attitudes were the reason she could not make her coffee farm a success. Her few supporters replied that her attitudes were the only reason Karen Coffee was still alive.

Chapter Seven

Leaving Africa

One of Denys Finch Hatton's greatest joys was his green and gold Gypsy Moth airplane. In 1930 he coaxed Dinesen into taking her first ride. He arrived while she was hosting a tea party. She protested that she could not leave her guests, but he promised to have her back before the tea cooled. She found his invitation so romantic she could not resist.

They took off in sunlight and headed toward the shade of the Ngong Hills. Looking out of the open-air plane, Dinesen could see the grasslands below and what looked like a wandering herd of insects. Hatton flew lower and they counted twenty-seven buffalo. The view from the plane was so revealing that it became a regular habit, every day before lunch, to go up and survey the landscape. Dinesen found the experience transporting and looked forward to her rides immensely.

These plane rides were among the few happy moments in her life. After nearly fourteen years of losing money, her family was determined to sell Karen Coffee to the first buyer. Dinesen continued to fight for her home and her way of life, but the family was determined. Their goal had been to make money, not to give her a pleasant place to live. She wrote letters home threatening to kill herself if the farm was sold, but instead of evoking sympathy, her threats only made the family fear she was becoming unstable in wild Africa and should return home.

Constant worry and depression endangered Dinesen's health. She had trouble eating and sleeping and lost sensation in her arms and legs. Sufferings from a combination of amebic dysentery, anemia, malnutrition, depression, and, as always, syphilis, she could barely think clearly. She would sometimes stop talking in the middle of a sentence, unable to remember what she meant to say. She felt paranoid, unable to trust those around her and acted alternately withdrawn or confrontational, and was always skittish and unpredictable. The natives described her as *kali*, a Swahili term meaning ferocious and erratic as a wild cat.

As the days went by, life on the farm seemed to get worse instead of better. Dinesen lost two good friends, including Hatton's best friend Berkeley Cole, to heart attacks. A swarm of locusts invaded, descending on the farm and stripping it bare. Finally, in 1931, the family wrote to inform Dinesen they had found a buyer for the Karen Coffee Company. She was going to lose her home.

Trips to Nairobi became an ordeal. Dinesen was practically destitute and could feel the stares of the Europeans she encountered there. She had sold most of her beautiful dresses and went to town in torn, unraveling sweaters and cracked shoes. She began staying closer to home, retreating to the place she felt safest.

Dinesen clung to Farah's children as if they were living security blankets. During the day, she carried his baby daughter everywhere she went. When nightmares kept her awake, Farah agreed to let his three-year-old son, Saufe, sleep beside her. The child's soft, steady breathing eased her agitated mind.

The final sale of the farm occurred in the middle of March 1931. Dinesen did not attend. A young real estate investor, Remi Martin, purchased the property in order to subdivide it and build houses. The Dinesen family signed the papers in Denmark on April 1, 1931. The amount they received for the farm did not even cover the legal fees incurred in selling it.

Before Dinesen would leave Africa and her beloved farm she was committed to finding a place for her workers to live. By law, the natives who worked and lived on the farm could only remain there for six months after it was sold. Yet the Kikuyu had lived on the land for many generations and their families knew no other home. The authorities recommended that Dinesen let each man fend for himself and his family. But that would mean disbanding the close-knit tribe.

After the sale the workers gathered around Dinesen's house every morning and stood there until nightfall. They were waiting for the news that she had secured

Farah, Dinesen's unfailingly loyal personal attendant, with his two sons. *(Courtesy of the Royal Library, Copenhagen.)*

them a place to live. She made numerous trips to town and the Governor's office, spending hours waiting, haggling, and pleading her case. It took months for an answer to come.

In April of 1931, Hatton returned to the farm for a visit. By this time, Dinesen had sold most of her belongings and packed away the mementos that she would take back to Denmark. His presence was upsetting to her; he found her neediness suffocating. They exchanged harsh words and Hatton left to stay with a friend in Nairobi. The couple soon made up and he returned to the farm. When he took off in his plane on May 8, she was already looking forward to his return.

When Hatton's plane did not come back on May 14 as he had promised, Dinesen asked Farah to keep a look out for him and went into town. There, she became convinced everyone was trying to avoid her. When her friends saw her approach, they hurried to their cars and drove away. She stopped for groceries and the usually friendly grocer blanched and left the store. Dinesen found a group of friends at a popular lunch place. Everyone there seemed sullen and no one wanted to talk to her. When she finished her meal, her friend Lady McMillan escorted her into a small sitting room and instructed her to sit down. There had been an accident, she told the bewildered woman. Hatton had crashed his plane. It burst into flames when it hit the ground. He was dead.

The shock and grief were so powerful, she sank into an almost catatonic state. She stayed in Nairobi where her friends could watch her. Each day she returned to their favorite club and sat in Hatton's old chair, not speaking to anyone. When she accepted an invitation to dinner, her friends thought it was a good sign. After the meal, she went to the bathroom and slashed her wrists. But her suicide attempt failed and the bleeding was stopped without a trip to the hospital.

Even in the midst of her grief Dinesen insisted on arranging Hatton's funeral. She and Farah rode up the Ngong Hills until they found a flat, breezy area covered in lush grass. It was only about five miles from Mbogani. The funeral service was brief but well attended and for a few days Mbogani was alive with people who had come to pay their respects.

When the last of the mourners left, Dinesen was once again alone. The grass began to grow back over Hatton's grave, so she collected large white stones to place there as markers. After a while, a lion and lioness began to appear near his grave at sunrise and sunset. It was an unusual sight, but did not surprise her. She thought it a fitting end for a man whose soul, like hers, belonged to Africa. For the rest of her time there, Dinesen gazed toward the Ngong Hills every night before she went to bed.

After the funeral, Dinesen resumed her efforts to secure land for her workers. Her trips into Nairobi were doubly hard now. The stares she had been so conscious of before were replaced by looks of pity, which were even worse. Knowing the humiliation she felt, Farah accompanied Dinesen on every trip and gave her the support she needed. He wore his finest gold-embroidered Arab waistcoats and colorful silk turbans. Erect and proud, he walked through the streets of Nairobi a few steps behind, a warrior protecting her as she fought for the people of her farm. In Dinesen's time of all-consuming loss and failure, Farah honored her with dignity.

The Governor granted Dinesen what would normally have been the impossible. He guaranteed her workers a plot of land in a nearby Kikuyu reserve where all two hundred families could live. They could even take with them their three thousand head of cattle. Dinesen and the Kikuyu were enormously happy and relieved.

Her house was emptied, her friends and neighbors were gone, and all Dinesen had left were her animals. She considered shooting them, but instead decided to give them away. A friend with a farm took her two deerhounds and promised they would always have room to run. She rode her favorite horse, Rouge, to the train station and helped secure him in a car. She rubbed her hand and cheek against his long face for the last time, then stepped back to watch the train carry away the last remnant of all she held dear in Africa.

An old friend, Ingrid Lindstrom, came to stay with Dinesen during her last few days on the empty farm. They did not discuss much, but Lindstrom listened as they walked the farm together and Dinesen described everything she saw as it had once been. She was saying goodbye.

Stress and the long-term effects of the doses of arsenic Dinesen took as treatment for syphilis had rav-aged her. Her hair fell out in clumps. She had lost her father, her health, her husband, her lover, her farm, and most of her friends. Now she was losing Africa. Physi-cally and spiritually drained, Dinesen watched as the last of her things were taken to the railway station. At the end of July 1931, she said goodbye to the few Africans left around the farm. To show her they wanted her to come back one day, they left the front door of her house open as she rode away.

In Nairobi, a few friends gathered to see her off. Farah went with her as far as Mombasa. Then Dinesen began the last leg of her journey as she had begun the first—alone and uncertain of what the future would bring.

Chapter Eight

Another New Life

On August 31, 1931, Karen Dinesen returned to Denmark to live with her mother in her childhood home, Rungstedlund. For seventeen years she had been an independent woman running a large farm and living in an exotic land. Now, she was back where she had begun and little seemed to have changed. While Dinesen and her mother were still close, many of her relatives, especially those who had invested in the Karen Coffee Company, were not as happy to see her.

Some of her relatives compared her to the prodigal son. Just like the father in the biblical story, they thought Ingeborg Dinesen was welcoming back a selfish child who squandered their money. A few cousins considered Dinesen proud and willful, and they gloated over her failure in Africa.

Dinesen's homecoming was made worse by another bout of illness. Her symptoms might have been a resurgence of syphilis, but were more likely the result of mercury and arsenic poisoning. Dosages of both were commonly prescribed to syphilis patients. Low doses do not have an immediate negative effect, but continued ingestion can cause a build-up of the poison in a person's body. Dinesen suffered from crippling stomach pain as well as pain in her lower back. She was often unable to eat solid foods and spent much of her time in bed.

Physical pain brought Dinesen down, and emotional pain kept her there. She was still grieving for the loss of her farm as well as for Denys Finch Hatton. Dinesen had looked for a way out of her bourgeois life for years. Now she was middle-aged and back where she started, once again alone. She struggled to cope with these losses as well as with the secret of her illness. Because syphilis is a venereal disease it carried with it a stigma. Though she contracted syphilis from an unfaithful husband, Dinesen was reluctant to share the truth about her health with anyone but her closest family members.

Just as she had as a young girl, Dinesen now coped with her pain and confusion by turning to writing. "If I had kept the farm," she later admitted, "I would never have become a writer." Remembering the story of the man who stumbled and fell only to create, unwittingly, a beautiful picture in the snow, Dinesen saw her losses as the price she had to pay in order to become an artist. At the age of forty-six, she was no longer an innocent little girl: "I promised the Devil my soul," she said wryly. "He gave me the gift of being able to transform everything that happened to me into a story."

The first story Dinesen wrote at Rungstedlund was "The Dreamers," which was published in *Seven Gothic Tales*. The story features three men on a ship approaching Mombasa, telling stories to pass the time. The setting is exotic, and the writing is full of rich and romantic detail told with a sly humor. One character, an Englishman with a restless spirit, narrates a tale about a woman he once knew.

The story he tells describes a woman, Pellegrina, who was the most famous and talented opera singer in the world. One night there is a fire on stage during a performance and she is badly burned. Taken home to recover, she awakens to realize she cannot sing a single note. Pellegrina tries to kill herself but does not succeed. She will see only one trusted friend who she insists must announce her death to the world. Pellegrina cannot be Pellegrina if she cannot sing. Her friend promises to help.

The news of her death is made public. Pellegrina tells her friend she has come to a great realization. She must forge a new life. She leaves her town, her friend, and her home to take a new name and become a new person. From the ashes of her former life she rises again, like the mythical Phoenix. The lesson of the story is that no one has to be just one person during the course of her life. When Pellegrina finds herself unable to sing, she simply stops being a singer and makes herself into someone else.

"The Dreamers" is an important story for Dinesen because it represents her certainty that something good would come of her life. At her lowest point, her gift was to be able to see hope in her future. Her stumbling might yet be part of a beautiful pattern.

Dinesen's writing was therapeutic. She set herself a goal of finishing a book within two years' time. Her mother was supportive, offering two rooms where she could work: Wilhelm's old office on the ground floor and Thomas's study upstairs. Ingeborg made sure the house was quiet while her daughter was writing. At Dinesen's request, Ingeborg turned away all visitors who arrived while Karen was working.

Dinesen wrote her stories in English, the language she had used to tell them originally on those nights in Africa when she, Hatton, and Berkeley Cole would settle in for an elegant dinner with fine wine and beautiful music. The two men would listen as she recounted the stories she had prepared for their visit. Dinesen transported herself back to that time and wrote as if she were speaking to the two men. She imagined Hatton as her muse, the inspiration for her imagination, and Cole as her artistic mentor. These two ghosts guided her pen.

Remembering how Cole savored style and cherished excellence, Dinesen strove for perfection on every page. Working on a typewriter meant entire pages had to be retyped in order to change one word—Dinesen did so regularly. When the pain in her abdomen forced her to stop, she would lie down on the floor and draw her knees up, the only position that offered any respite. There, she would continue to polish her story in her head. When the pain abated, she would resume typing.

This page is from a draft of an article Dinesen was writing about the Masai. Primarily a nomadic herding people, the Masai have been quite resistant to the cultural shifts taking place in Africa. Dinesen became fascinated by the Masai, some of whom lived near her African farm. *(Courtesy of the Royal Library, Copenhagen.)*

Dinesen learned the importance of revision to her work, writing draft after draft to make a story as tightly woven as possible.

She finished her first collection of stories, *Seven Gothic Tales*, in the spring of 1933. After some deliberation, Dinesen chose a pen name, Isak, which means "one who laughs." It is the name the biblical couple Sarah and Abraham gave to the child they finally had in their old age. Dinesen meant the name to be partly ironic and partly serious. Her writing was the belated reward of her life, and while her health kept her from the adventures she still longed for, her spirit refused to suffer.

Finding a publisher for her book was difficult. Her brother Thomas introduced her to an American author, Dorothy Canfield Fisher, who read and loved the book. Fisher recommended it to her New York publisher, Robert Haas, who was impressed by her talent but reluctant to publish a book in America written by an unknown European.

Dinesen took her manuscript to London and attempted to show it to Constant Huntington, an editor at Putnam's publishing house. He refused even to look at it. Undaunted, Dinesen went back to Haas, sending him two more stories. She won him over, and he agreed to publish the book.

Haas wanted Dinesen to publish under her own name, but she insisted on the pseudonym. She needed to have some distance from her work—she dreaded the idea of critics and reviewers demanding to know where the

The 1934 photograph that introduced Isak Dinesen to the world.
(Courtesy of Reimert Kehlet.)

stories came from and whether she had actually experienced what she wrote. Later, Dinesen would come to peace with the past and feel more comfortable talking about her work, but the publication of her first book made her nervous.

The first printing came out in America in 1934 and was an immediate success. Critics at first thought the author was a European man, just as Dinesen had hoped. They were impressed that the author had set the book in the age of George Gordon, Lord Byron, who had died almost one hundred years before. Byron was associated with the Gothic or Romantic style Dinesen imitated in these tales. They are best described as tales, rather than stories, because they shun excess narration in order to focus on the experiences of the characters. These seven tales recount the often-eerie adventures of a wild collection of sailors and noblemen and brave but tormented women. Each person succumbs to Dinesen's conviction that one's fate cannot be escaped.

Seven Gothic Tales became a Book-of-the-Month Club selection and fifty thousand copies were printed at once. News of the book spread rapidly and soon the press was clamoring to meet and talk to Isak Dinesen. Haas convinced Dinesen she could safely introduce herself to the world. She gave her first interview to the journal *Politiken*. A photo that revealed the real Isak Dinesen appeared with the interview. It was a full-length portrait of a slim, elegant woman wearing a draped white chiffon dress. Dinesen stands sideways to the camera, her head is tilted down, and her eyes appear to be closed. She is smiling, faintly, and her hands are held at her waist. The impression is of a private, even mysterious, woman who allows the photographer his moment but is on her way to some other place.

The book's success in America brought European publishers into a bidding war. Constant Huntington, at Putnam, read the book and loved it. He was quick to secure the British rights, never realizing that it was the same book he had rejected without reading a few months before. Dinesen was delighted to get a letter from him full of praise and offering a generous contract.

The only readers who were not captivated by the book seemed to be the people of Dinesen's own country. Once her identity was revealed, critics took her to task for what they saw as her allegiance to an out-dated class system. Her family had money while the Danish people were suffering from the effects of the Great Depression that gripped Europe and the United States. There was an unemployment rate of almost forty percent in Denmark. They thought her work frivolous and inappropriate at such a time.

Danish critic Frederick Schyberg wrote a scathing review in which he called the entire work perverse. He saw the author as a shallow, capricious, false, name-dropping snob. He told his readers Dinesen was hiding behind a veil of strange characters and unbelievable situations and that if the veil was lifted the readers would find nothing there. Dinesen cut out the review and kept it for the rest of her life. Years later, she would bring it out to show to friends and ask them to listen as

Ingeborg Dinesen and Karen at a 1935 celebration for the Danish publication of *Seven Gothic Tales. (Courtesy of the Royal Library, Copenhagen.)*

she read from it, as if she still could not believe the words he had written.

Dinesen encountered more trouble in Denmark when her work was to be translated. She contracted a Danish firm but was unhappy with their efforts and finally decided to do the job herself. She thought the decision was only logical since Danish was her native language, but people in the publishing industry were amazed. Very few authors ever do their own translations—it is simply too difficult. Dinesen's translations were excellent and vaulted her into a rarified company of authors who can write with great skill in two languages.

Danish readers would eventually come to claim Dinesen as their greatest living author, but by then it was too late. She was wary of their praise and always felt slighted by her own country. Her real home would always be Africa.

In 1935, Italian Fascist dictator Benito Mussolini ordered his army to invade Ethiopia in Northern Africa. Dinesen, desperate to return to Africa, petitioned every news organization she could find for a job as a war correspondent. Though she had experience on the continent, they all turned her down. She tried to gain permission from the government to travel there on her own, but was told it was too dangerous for a woman. Frustrated and angry, Dinesen traveled to Geneva, Switzerland, where the League of Nations was meeting to discuss Mussolini's actions. There she listened to speeches by day and was entertained in cabarets by night. She was glad to be involved in the conflict, even if only in this peripheral way.

Dinesen received the strange news that her ex-husband, Bror, was planning to write his memoirs. He sent her a brief note from Africa to update her on old friends like Farah, who still traveled with him, and to let her know that he was working with a ghostwriter on a book. Dinesen was surprised and nervous at the news. Bror had never seemed to value literature very highly and she worried he would use the occasion to attack her. Her fears went unrealized, as Bror's book made little mention of his first wife. It did, however, make Dinesen give more thought to writing a book of her own about Africa.

For the past few years, Dinesen had been making notes and writing brief sketches about her life in Africa. It was an extremely difficult subject for her to face because of the emotions it brought up. She was reluctant to write about Africa, but her brother Thomas urged her to pursue the subject, insisting it would be healing for her. It was either that, he told her dryly, or get religion. Dinesen knew he meant for her to find a sense of peace or acceptance by acknowledging the events of her past. She began to write in earnest.

Out of Africa is a highly emotional memoir that captures Dinesen's memories of the place she prized above all others. The book is usually considered to be her masterpiece. *Out of Africa* begins "I had a farm in Africa, at the foot of the Ngong Hills." The rest is filled with reminiscences about her time there. Part fact, part fiction, the book reads more like a diary than a novel. It is episodic, not following any single storyline. Characters and landscapes are given rich description and colorization, from the stately and majestic Farah to the nimble and impetuous Lulu.

While Dinesen recounts the beauty and happiness she found in Africa, she does not shy away from the death and hardship she encountered there either. The details of her relationships with Bror and Hatton are not discussed, nor is the source of her illness. Just as Dinesen's gothic tales were set one hundred years back in time, *Out of Africa* reads as though it were a story from the past. It is a romanticized account of Dinesen's

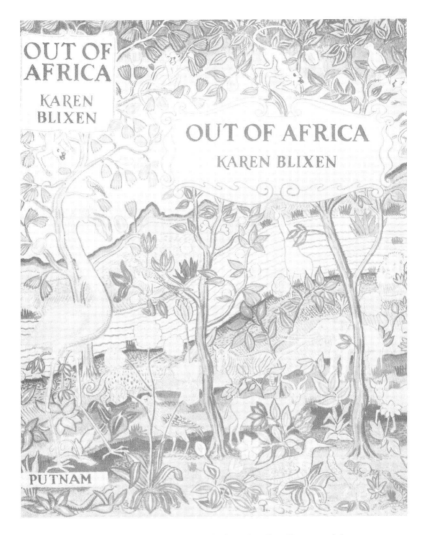

The cover for the British version of *Out of Africa.* Random House used the same cover when it published the book in the United States. Dinesen actually preferred the cover of the original Danish version, which was based on an African drawing that Dinesen's cook, Esa, had given her as a gift. *(Courtesy of the Royal Library, Copenhagen.)*

life on the farm that seems almost like a dream.

Dinesen's descriptions of Africa are so lush and rich the landscapes almost rise up off the page. Many of her readers were drawn to the book because of its novelty. They wanted to know more about the woman who had lived such an exciting and adventurous life. It is inspirational because it upholds Dinesen's conviction that beauty can come of tragedy. Now considered to be one of the best examples ever of the pastoral narrative, it was released in 1937 and became an instant success.

Two years later, in January of 1939, Ingeborg Dinesen died, at the age of eighty-five. While the loss of her mother was difficult, it also meant Dinesen now had a certain freedom for the first time in her life. She was financially secure, had a place of her own to live, and was doing well in her career. But just as she began to enjoy this new period of her life a new war brought everyone's happiness to an end.

On September 1, Germany invaded Poland. Two days later, Dinesen went to the offices of *Politiken*, the journal that had published her first interview as Isak Dinesen, and begged for work as a journalist. She wanted to be a part of the conflict that was developing across Western Europe. The editor at *Politiken* agreed and suggested she visit Berlin, Paris, and London, the capitals of the three major nations at war, and write four articles from each.

Dinesen set out for Berlin. She had no connections there but because she was a journalist, the Ministry of Propaganda gave her a warm welcome. Dinesen was not sympathetic to the Nazis but did her best to report objectively on what she saw. Her tours of the country were scheduled and chaperoned by the government, and she was frustrated not to get a look at what was really going on. The idea of meeting with Nazi leaders made her uncomfortable and she refused their invitations. The resultant series of articles was critical of Nazism but limited in its scope by Dinesen's inexperience as a journalist and her inability to see anything other than what the Germans wanted her to.

The next stop on her journey was supposed to be London, but Dinesen's career as a journalist was cut short when Germany invaded Denmark on April 9, 1940.

At the time of the invasion Rungstedlund was empty except for Dinesen. She spent the war years there, largely alone. Gasoline was rationed, making travel all but impossible, and blackout conditions were in effect at night. Dinesen moved into the low-ceilinged west wing of the big house where she drew heat from wood-burning stoves and spent her days writing. She saw friends and bicycled around the countryside, but the early war years was mainly devoted to the production of her third book, *Winter's Tales*, published in 1942.

Winter's Tales is a nod to Shakespeare's play *A Winter's Tale* in which a character says "a sad tale's best for winter." The book is the most Danish of all her works; it is a quiet, melancholy piece. Among the stories is "Sorrow-acre," a tragic yarn derived from a seventeenth-century South Jutland folktale about a peasant woman who dies trying to save her son from execution.

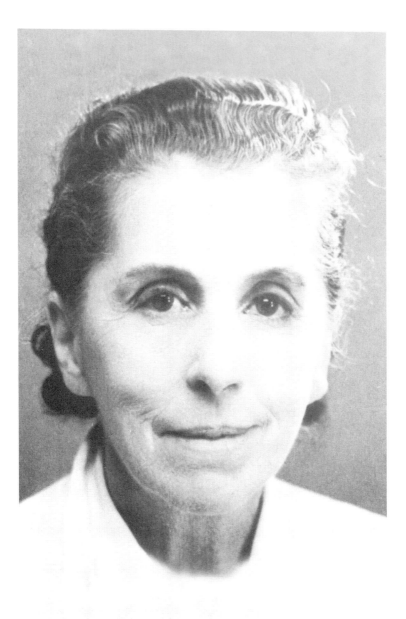

Dinesen in 1940. *(Courtesy of Johannes Øvereng.)*

Most critics and scholars consider "Sorrow-acre" her best short work for two reasons. Technically, the story builds momentum as it accelerates toward its heartbreaking climax. Characters, who serve both as individuals and personifications of different philosophies, interact to set a mood and contribute to the fate of the mother and son. Thematically, it combines wit, grace, and pathos to express Dinesen's belief that proud people find happiness by fulfilling their destinies. In the story, the noble yet tragic price of this fulfillment makes the conclusion both uplifting and devastating.

Besides releasing the usual hardbound version, her publisher also printed a special Armed Services edition of *Winter's Tales* that fit into the pocket of army fatigues. Dinesen learned the extent of her popularity when an American soldier wrote her a letter saying that he and his comrades had been carrying her book with them across Germany and the Philippines. She was glad to hear that her writing had touched the souls of the kind of men she most admired—those willing to risk their lives for a cause.

Lives were at stake much closer to Dinesen's home when the occupying Germans made secret plans to round up eight thousand Danish Jews and take them to a concentration camp. A strong underground Resistance in Denmark discovered the plan and a copy of the list of names. The Danish people rallied together in defense of their friends and neighbors. Strangers offered strangers sanctuary in their homes; ministers spoke out against aiding the Nazis. When the Germans came knocking on doors to begin the roundup, over seven thousand Danish Jews had disappeared. They were hidden all over the country until they could be transported to Sweden, which was neutral and had reluctantly agreed to accept the refugees.

From Dinesen's balcony she could see the Swedish coast. She volunteered her home as one of the staging points for the exodus and, like her countrymen, was proud to stand up against the Nazis. Almost all of the Danish Jews made it safely to Sweden.

The war took an enormous toll on Europe. Dinesen felt the anguish as keenly as she felt the pain from her degenerating spine. She could muster little enthusiasm for beginning another deep, introspective work. Her next book was a light, historical crime novel, *The Angelic Avengers*. The finished piece was so unlike her earlier work she published it under a different pseudonym, Pierre Andrézel. The book, written in Danish, was not a great success, but it sold well enough to warrant an English translation.

In 1945 the war finally ended. The people of Europe began to take stock of their losses and to rebuild. Dinesen was still at Rungstedlund, where, at the age of sixty, she found that the pain in her abdomen and lower back prevented her from taking care of herself. She could no longer even sit up or write on her own. She hired a shy twenty-eight-year-old named Clara Svendsen to be her full-time cook, housemaid, and secretary. While lying flat on the floor to help ease some of her back pain, Dinesen dictated everything else she wrote, beginning with the English version of *The Angelic Avengers*. The novel was only a minor success and was her first book not chosen as a Book-of-the-Month Club selection.

Svendsen was drawn to Dinesen because of her respect for her books. She volunteered herself to cook, clean, and type, all for the chance to be in the presence of her idol. She was the first of several admirers to seek out Dinesen's company, which pleased Dinesen enormously. Younger poets and writers asked her to comment on their work. She often invited them to Rungstedlund, where she received visitors as if at court.

One young poet, Thorkild Bjørnvig, became a particular favorite. He had just finished his master's degree and was married, with a young son. Dinesen sought out his company and the two began to spend almost all their time together. Dinesen was a great champion of Bjørnvig's work and tried hard to infuse him with confidence. In turn, he came to admire her enormously and was proud to be the object of her attention.

After he experienced an emotional breakdown, Dinesen invited Bjørnvig to Rungstedlund to recover. They grew even closer while he was there. Dinesen and Bjørnvig made what they called a pact—she would protect him and nurture his poetry if he would devote himself to her. Many years before Dinesen had said she had made a pact with the devil that he would give her talent in exchange for her soul. Now, she reenacted that pact with Bjørnvig, playing the role of the devil herself.

Outsiders, including Bjørnvig's wife, found their relationship odd. Dinesen was the happiest she had been since Denys Finch Hatton died—she had the undivided devotion and respect of a man she admired. She tried to mold Bjørnvig into the kind of man she thought he could be. "Be hard," she told him, "only hard things ring...A string on a violin is...hard, so is a bowstring, also a rather thin crystal glass can ring if it was hard enough to stand the grinding." Bjørnvig fell under her spell and obeyed her every instruction. He would wear flowers in his hair when she told him to; he went abroad at her command. For four years, he was at her mercy.

Finally, Dinesen asked too much of him. One Christmas, she expected Bjørnvig to stay with her at Rungstedlund, but he wanted to be with his family. He disobeyed her wishes and began the long and painful process of extricating himself from her life. Dinesen was reluctant to let him go, but Bjørnvig's fascination with her had run its course. His loss was a blow. They tried several times to reconcile to some degree but were unable. They parted barely on speaking terms.

Bjørnvig's absence left a hole in Dinesen's life during a period of great success. Her books were selling well and she had plenty of money. But there was little to spend that money on in post-war Europe—good food was still scarce, and her illness prevented her from traveling. Over the next years her health continued to deteriorate and she was frequently in and out of the hospital. Doctors tried several radical surgeries, including severing some of the nerves of her spinal cord, but her pain persisted.

Despite the pain, Dinesen continued to write. In the

Poet Thorkild Bjørnvig and Dinesen, about 1950. For a time, Bjørnvig would fill the place left vacant in Dinesen's life since Denys Finch Hatton's death. *(Courtesy of the Royal Library, Copenhagen.)*

1950s she developed a professional relationship with the editors of the American magazine, *Ladies' Home Journal*, who began publishing the new stories she dictated to Clara. Her first submission, "Babette's Feast," expanded her already huge fan base in the United States and made Dinesen want to travel there at least once before she died.

The first of many broadcasts on Danish radio helped to secure Dinesen's popularity in her home country.

Almost always, she talked about her life in Africa. Her deep voice and entrancing stories captured the country's imagination.

Her acclaim reached its zenith in the mid-1950s. Dinesen received two nominations for writing's highest honor, the Nobel Prize for Literature. In 1954, she lost to American author Ernest Hemingway, but her loss came with a much-appreciated acknowledgment. Like her, Hemingway hunted game in Africa. He did not know her personally, but he had gone on safaris with Bror, and he loved Dinesen's writing. In response to his win, Hemingway said that he thought the prize really should have been awarded to "that beautiful writer Isak Dinesen."

During a 1957 interview, Swedish journalist Anders Lundebeck told Dinesen that she had been nominated for the Nobel Prize again. He was sure she was the favorite to win. Lundebeck's compliment left her especially disappointed when the prize went to French existentialist novelist and philosopher Albert Camus.

Dinesen continued to write with passion well into her seventies. Her final collection of stories appeared in November of 1957 under the title *Last Tales*. Her next book, *Anecdotes of Destiny* was mostly a compilation of stories published in *Ladies' Home Journal*.

Dinesen matched her frantic work pace with a strenuous social life. She traveled as often as her health allowed, often returning to Rungstedlund completely drained, taking to her bed until she had the strength to stand again, then moving on. Increasingly, she relied on amphetamines to keep her energy up. She ate very little, smoked almost nonstop, and frequently collapsed. Clara Svendsen became used to finding her employer passed out from exhaustion or having to carry her when Dinesen could not walk. She was anemic, emaciated, malnourished, and yet, strangely, alive.

Chapter Nine

Swan Song

Clara Svendsen gave over her life to the care of her irascible mistress. As Dinesen's physical suffering increased, she often berated Clara, then moments later either apologized or seemed not even to remember having verbally assaulting her. No matter how irrational and venomous Dinesen's pain made her, Svendsen remained loyal to her for the rest of her life. Afterward, she protected Dinesen's legacy by becoming her literary executor and administering the artistic and financial rights for all Dinesen's works.

In 1959, Dinesen was seventy-three years old. Dr. Alvin Eurich of the Ford Foundation's Fund for the Advancement of Knowledge asked her to read and discuss her work for a series they were filming about the world's greatest living writers. He invited her to the United States—all expenses paid—but offered to come to Denmark if she could not travel. Dinesen immediately replied to say she would come to America. She had longed to travel to the United States for many years, ever since she first heard her father's stories. In order to make the visit profitable, she inquired through her publishers whether anyone might be interested in inviting her to lecture. She was deluged by offers.

Svendsen was apprehensive about the trip. She feared Dinesen would push herself too hard. The author had spent the previous winter almost completely bedridden and her health was fragile. Dinesen was filled with excitement about the journey, which made Svendsen more apprehensive—Dinesen's enthusiasm often took a toll on her already precarious health. They planned a trip of nearly four months.

Dinesen's popularity in America had not waned since the publication of *Seven Gothic Tales* and for many reasons she had long considered Americans to be her true readership. She wrote almost all of her books in English and saw them published in America before she translated them to Danish. She had several unpleasant encounters with Danish critics and audiences that left her permanently soured on those readers. Americans, she felt, truly appreciated her work.

Isak Dinesen was in great demand in America. Thousands of people came to hear her speak and were transfixed from their first views of the author. She was incredibly thin and the skin of her face hung in sharp folds. Her voice was, as always, deep and strangely beautiful. Her eyes were deep set and held the sparkle she kept through years of illness and loss. She seemed unimaginably old, yet she spoke with a power and eloquence that mesmerized audiences. Readers who felt as though they knew her from her stories and *Out of Africa* had their sense of a strong, elegant, refined but defiant woman confirmed.

Dinesen refused to read from her work. She was not, she said, a reader. She was a storyteller. So she took to the stage and recounted, from memory, stories she had written, word for word. Audience members were amazed to find she never deviated from the printed version of

Clara Svendsen and Dinesen on an airplane bound for New York in January 1959. Dinesen spent four event-filled months in the United States, returning home to Denmark exhausted but happy on her seventy-fourth birthday, April 17, 1959. *(Courtesy of Kaj Lund Hansen.)*

the story—her excellent memory had not failed.

At the annual meeting of the American Academy, Dinesen gave the keynote speech. She took as her theme "On Mottoes of My Life" and used the occasion to look back over the past seventy-four years. Dinesen expressed clearly for her listeners the passage her life had taken. She traced her experiences from an unhappy, restless childhood to a free and passionate life in Africa, the desperate return to Denmark, and finally to her old age, where she found wisdom and strength.

After the speech, she was seated at a table with the American writer Carson McCullers. McCullers had long admired Dinesen and sought out a chance to meet her. The two were linked by their genius in writing and by the diseases that disabled them. McCullers had suffered rheumatic fever as a child that left her unwell the rest of her life. A few days after the meeting, McCullers hosted a dinner whose guests included playwright Arthur Miller and his wife at the time, Marilyn Monroe. Dinesen was as captivated by Monroe as she had once been by the lion cubs she saw in Africa.

There was no shortage of invitations to be the guest of honor at parties and events. Barbara Paley, wife of the founder of the Columbia Broadcasting System, invited luminaries such as the writers Truman Capote and Cecil Beaton to a luncheon honoring Dinesen at the St. Regis hotel. Heiress Gloria Vanderbilt and director Sidney Lumet brought her to their penthouse for dinner. Afterward, Lumet carried her around the terrace in his arms so she could see the lights of the city. She even

The playwright Arthur Miller, his wife Marilyn Monroe, the author Carson McCullers, and Dinesen, enjoying lunch together at McCullers' New Jersey home in 1959. Dinesen and McCullers each held the other's writing in great esteem. *(Courtesy of the Royal Library, Copenhagen.)*

heard opera star Maria Callas sing *Il Pirata* and was mobbed by fans on Fifty-seventh Street.

Clara Svendsen found herself in the difficult position of having to say no to her employer. Dinesen could not be forced to eat, she would barely sleep, and always wanted more company, conversation, and excitement. Svendsen tried to rein her in but succeeded at doing little besides earning Dinesen's wrath. Helpless, Svendsen could only watch as her idol drove herself to destruction.

In February, Dinesen had to be taken to the hospital. She was suffering from malnourishment and exhaustion. Doctors there ordered her to rest and recover her strength. They warned that if she did not, she probably would not survive the trip home. After a few weeks, she was released. Svendsen made reservations and on April 17, 1959, Dinesen's seventy-fourth birthday, the stubborn writer had no choice but to return to Denmark.

At home, Dinesen continued to visit friends as often as she could. She became more difficult and demanding. Finally Svendsen's concern proved too confining. In a stunning move, Dinesen fired her friend and companion of thirteen years. Svendsen understood that the decision was not entirely rational or personal, and she was glad for the time away. She had given over her life to Dinesen and was pleased to have some of it back. After a few months, they reconciled and Svendsen returned to Rungstedlund with the understanding that Dinesen would leave her alone at least on Sundays.

The last literary project of Dinesen's life was *Shadows on the Grass*. She and Svendsen began working on it in earnest in 1960, and it was published soon after— in Denmark that year and America the next. The work is meant to be a sequel to *Out of Africa* but does not have the quality of the original. *Shadows on the Grass* was created out of several pieces Dinesen had written over the years—some for radio, some published as stories, and others originally intended for *Out of Africa*.

Dictating, as always, to Svendsen, Dinesen added one new part, "Echoes from the Hills." It is the weakest

Dinesen and her brother Anders in 1960, at their great-grandfather's summer residence in Copenhagen. *(Courtesy of John Stewart.)*

section of the book. She knew it, and blamed the poor quality on her failing health and the distraction of renovations to Rungstedlund—in 1960, the manor received its first indoor toilet. *Shadows on the Grass* went to press with little of the fanfare of her previous works.

For the next two years Dinesen's health worsened. Still, she continued to travel and give talks. She wanted to make one last trip to Africa, but simply did not have the strength. She found reserves of energy that gave her a few happy days in Paris, with friends, and memorable times at home. Great figures from around the world came to Rungstedlund to pay their respects and she relished the attention. Until the very end, she welcomed visitors and sat for hours in her living room listening to and engaging in conversations.

On September 7, 1962, Karen Dinesen died, at home, with Clara Svendsen at her side. She was seventy-seven years old. The last photographs taken of her are from June of that year. They show a fragile, emaciated woman whose flesh hangs from her bones, but whose eyes still sparkle with her indomitable spirit. Four days after her death, a procession of family and friends followed Dinesen's horse-drawn coffin to the foot of Ewald's Hill. She was buried under a large beech tree, near where she had played as a child.

It is not known whether, if one viewed it from above, the pattern of Dinesen's wanderings on this earth would form the outline of a stork. But her conviction that her life would add up to something beautiful is borne out by the work she left behind. Her story "Babette's Feast"

Dinesen in New York City, 1959, in a photograph by Cecil Beaton. *(Courtesy of the Royal Library, Copenhagen.)*

was made into a movie of the same name and won an Academy Award for Best Foreign Film in 1987. *Out of Africa* also became a movie and took seven Academy Awards, including Best Picture, in 1985.

Isak Dinesen's works have received a good deal of scholarly attention over the years. There are many books written about her, and even a one-woman play. Her strength, courage, and all-too-human foibles continue to capture our hearts as her romantic, elevated, and precise prose captures our imaginations.

Timeline

1885   April 17: Karen Christentze Dinesen is born at Rungstedlund near Copenhagen, Denmark to father Wilhelm Dinesen and mother Ingeborg Westenholz Dinesen.

1895   March 28: Wilhelm Dinesen hangs himself from the rafters of a boardinghouse in Copenhagen, Denmark.

1899   On a six-month trip to Switzerland with her mother and sisters, Karen gets her first taste of life beyond Denmark and receives her first formal education.

1902   Karen takes drawing lessons at the Misses Meldahl and Sode's Art School in Copenhagen.

1904   Karen enrolls in the Academy of Art.

1907   "The Hermits," Dinesen's first published short story, appears in the August issue of the Copenhagen periodical *Tilskueren*, under the pseudonym Osceola. Dinesen's second published short story, "The Ploughman," under the same pen name, appears in the October issue of the periodical *Gads danske Magasin*.

1908   Dinesen falls in love with dashing distant cousin Hans von Blixen-Finecke.

1909   Another of Dinesen's stories, "The de Kats Family," is published in the January issue of *Tilskueren.*

1912   Accompanied by her sister Inger, Dinesen briefly attends art school in Paris. In December, Dinesen returns from Paris and agrees to marry Bror von Blixen-Finecke, a baron and the twin brother of Hans.

1913   December 2: Dinesen leaves Denmark to join Bror in British East Africa where they plan to run a coffee farm at the foot of the Ngong Hills.

1914   January 14: Upon her arrival in Africa, Dinesen marries Bror and acquires the title Baroness.
       Dinesen is diagnosed with syphilis, contracted from Bror.

1915   Doctors send Dinesen to Paris, then home to Denmark, to be treated for syphilis. While recuperating at Rungstedlund, Dinesen pines for Africa and writes the poem "Ex Africa."

1916   As World War I inflates coffee prices, Dinesen's family forms the Karen Coffee Company.

1917   January 12: Daisy Frijs, Dinesen's cousin and closest friend growing up, commits suicide.

1918   April 5: Dinesen meets and falls in love with free-spirited English aristocrat, Denys Finch Hatton.

1921   Aage Westenholz, Dinesen's uncle and the main share holder of the Karen Coffee Company, threatens to sell. Dinesen and Bror separate, and Bror moves to Nairobi.

1922   Dinesen becomes pregnant with Denys Finch Hatton's child, but miscarries only weeks later.

1924   Dinesen completes a long essay about the history of marriage she titles "Modern Marriage and Other Considerations."

1925   Dinesen and Bror's divorce becomes final.

1926   Dinesen miscarries another child by Denys.

1926 *The Revenge of Truth,* a play Dinesen wrote as a young girl, becomes her first work published under her own name.

1929 September: Dinesen takes her first flight over Africa with Denys.

1931 Uncle Aage and the family sell the Karen Coffee Company to Nairobi real estate developer Remi Martin, who names the district Karen in her honor. On May 14, Denys Fitch Hatten is killed when the plane he is piloting crashes in Tanganyika. In July, Dinesen leaves Africa and moves back to Rungstedlund.

1934 *Seven Gothic Tales,* by Isak Dinesen, is published in the United States, and then England.

1935 The Danish translation of *Seven Gothic Tales* is lambasted by critics and ignored by readers, leaving Dinesen forever bitter about her homeland.

1936 Dinesen begins writing her masterpiece, *Out of Africa.*

1937 *Out of Africa* and its Danish version, *The African Farm,* are published.

1939 January 27: Ingeborg Dinesen dies.

1942 *Winter's Tales* is published.

1944 Dinesen completes *The Angelic Avengers,* a historical crime novel she wrote in Danish. It is published under the pen name Pierre Andrézel.

1945 Dinesen hires Clara Svendsen to be her cook, housemaid, and secretary.

1948 Thorkild Bjørnvig, a young poet and ardent fan, begins visiting Rungstedlund.

1950 American magazine *Ladies' Home Journal* starts publishing Dinesen's stories, beginning with "Babette's Feast." Thorkild Bjørnvig moves to Rungstedlund.

1953 Bjørnvig ends their friendship.

1954   Dinesen is nominated for the Nobel Prize for Literature but loses to Ernest Hemingway.

1957   *Last Tales* is published in both English and Danish. Dinesen is again considered for the Nobel Prize and loses to Albert Camus.

1958   Dinesen helps establish the Rungstedlund Foundation which will safeguard the integrity of her work after her death and make the Rungstedlund estate a bird reserve and historic site open to the public. *Anecdotes of Destiny,* a compilation of mostly previously published stories, is released in America, England, and Denmark.

1959   Dinesen takes her lifelong dream trip to the United States, where she spends four months.

1960   *Shadows on the Grass,* a continuation of *Out of Africa,* is published in England and Denmark.

1961   *Shadows on the Grass* is released in America.

1962   September 7: Dinesen dies at Rungstedlund.

1963   "Ehrengard," the first of Dinesen's previously unprinted tales, is published in America, England, and Denmark.

1964   An anthology of Dinesen's writing is published as *Works.*

1965   A compilation of Dinesen's essays is published in Denmark as Karen Blixen's *Essays.*

1975   The rest of Dinesen's previously unpublished tales, some written in English, others in Danish, are released in Denmark as the book, *Posthumous Tales.*

1977   *Posthumous Tales,* reprinted under the title, *Carnival: Entertainments and Posthumous Tales,* is published in America and England.

1978   Dinesen's correspondence to family is compiled and published in Denmark as the book, *Letters from Africa 1914-1931.*

1979   *Daguerreotypes and Other Essays,* a compilation of the transcript from her famous radio speech about Rungstedlund and an English translation of the book, *Essays,* is published in America and England.

1981   *Letters from Africa 1914-1931* is published in America and England.

1985   Sydney Pollack's American motion picture adaptation of *Out of Africa* creates a huge resurgence of interest in Dinesen's writing.

1987   Gabriel Axel's acclaimed Danish film version of "Babette's Feast" attracts an international audience.

1991   Rungstedlund is opened to the public as a museum honoring the life and writings of Karen Blixen.

Sources

CHAPTER TWO: A Romantic Youth

p. 18, "as a kind of marionette play . . ." Eric O. Johannesson, *The World of Isak Dinesen* (Seattle: University of Washington Press, 1961), 81.

p. 20, "Just when one feels . . ." Isak Dinesen, *Letters from Africa, 1914-1931* (Chicago: University of Chicago Press, 1981), 49.

p. 22, "lift life out . . ." Ibid., 42.

p. 24, "a truly horrendous melancholy . . ." Judith Thurman, *Isak Dinesen: The Life of a Storyteller* (New York: Picador, 1982), 91. Thurman attributes these lines to "Paris Diary" (Dagborg) March 24-May 22, 1910, KBA 118, III a 4.

CHAPTER THREE: A New Life in a New Land

p. 30, "the sky was rarely more . . ." Isak Dinesen, *Out of Africa.* (New York: The Modern Library, 1985), 4.

p. 32, "dry and burnt . . ." Ibid., 3.

p. 32, "a mosaic of little . . ." Ibid., 5-6.

CHAPTER FOUR: Difficulty and Illness

p. 46, "there are two things . . ." Thurman, *Isak Dinesen,* 138.

CHAPTER FIVE: Life in Africa

p. 54, "You *must* take great care . . ." Dinesen, *Letters from Africa,* 80-81.

p. 56, "If I live to be seventy . . ." Ibid., 82.

p. 56, "most fervently beg . . ." Ibid.

p. 62, "Msabu . . . I think you had better . . ." Dinesen, *Out of Africa,* 42.

CHAPTER SIX: Making a Home

p. 64, "ideal . . ." Dinesen, *Letters from Africa,* 89

p. 66, "Let us go . . ." Dinensen, *Out of Africa,* 241.

p. 68, "the joy of my life," Dinesen, Isak. *Letters from Africa,* 286.

p. 68, " I believe that for all time . . ." Dinesen, Ibid., 224.

CHAPTER EIGHT: Another New Life

p. 83, "If I had kept the farm . . ." Johannesson, *The World of Isak Dinesen,* 5.

p. 83, "I promised the Devil .. ." Thorkild Bjørnvig, *The Pact: My Friendship with Isak Dinesen* (New York: St. Martin's Press, 1983), 50.

p. 83, "He gave me the gift . . ." Aage Henriksen, *Isak Dinesen – Karen Blixen: The Work and the Life* (New York: St. Martin's Press, 1988), 126.

p. 93, "I had a farm . . ." Dinesen, *Out of Africa,* 3.

p. 101, "Be hard . . ." Bjørnvig, *The Pact,* 49.

p. 103, "that beautiful writer . . ." Ernest Hemingway, *Selected Letters, 1917-1961* (New York: Charles Scribner, 1980), 839.

Major Works

(In order of publication)

Dinesen, Isak. *Seven Gothic Tales*. New York: Harrison Smith and Robert Haas, 1934; London: Putnam, 1934.

Dinesen, Isak. *Out of Africa*. London: Putnam, 1937; New York: Random House, 1938.

Dinesen, Isak. *Winter's Tales*. New York: Random House; London: Putnam, 1942.

Andrézel, Pierre. *The Angelic Avengers*. Copenhagen: Gyldenhal, 1944.

Dinesen, Isak. *Last Tales*. New York: Random House; London: Putnam, 1957.

Dinesen, Isak. *Anecdotes of Destiny*. New York: Random House; London: Michael Joseph, 1958.

Dinesen, Isak. *Shadows on the Grass*. New York: Random House; London: Michael Joseph, 1961.

Dinesen, Isak. *Ehrengard*. New York: Random House; London: Michael Joseph, 1963.

Blixen, Karen. *Essays*. Copenhagen: Gyldendal, 1965.

Dinesen, Isak. *Carnival: Entertainments and Posthumous Tales*. Chicago: University of Chicago Press, 1977.

Bibliography

Bever, Edward. *Africa*. Phoenix, AZ: Oryx, 1996.

Bjørnvig, Thorkild. *The Pact: My Friendship with Isak Dinesen*. Translated from the Danish by Ingvar Schousboe. New York: St. Martin's Press, 1983.

Davidson, Basil. *Africa in History*. New York: Touchstone, 1991.

Dinesen, Isak. *Anecdotes of Destiny and Ehringard*. New York: Vintage, 1985.

———. *Herself Telling Two Stories*. Auburn, California: Audio Editions, 1988.

———. *An Isak Dinesen Feast*. Auburn, California: Audio Partners, 1997.

———. *Isak Dinesen's Africa*. New York: Bantam, 1985.

———. *Letters from Africa, 1914-1931*. Translated by Anne Born. Chicago: University of Chicago Press, 1981.

———. *Last Tales*. New York: Vintage, 1991.

———. *Out of Africa*. New York: The Modern Library, 1985.

———. *Seven Gothic Tales*. Introduction by Dorothy Canfield. New York: The Modern Library, 1994.

———. *Shadows on the Grass*. New York: Random House, 1974.

────. *Winter's Tales.* New York: Vintage, 1993.

Dinesen, Thomas. *My Sister, Isak Dinesen.* Translated by Joan Tate. London: Michael Joseph, 1975.

Donelson, Linda. *Karen Blixen—Isak Dinesen.* 22 October 2002 <http://www.karenblixen.com>

Donelson, Linda. *Out of Isak Dinesen in Africa: Karen Blixen's Untold Story.* Iowa City, IA: Coulsong, 1998.

Hemingway, Ernest, *Selected Letters, 1917-1961.* Carlos Baker, ed. New York: Charles Scribner, 1980.

Henriksen, Aage. *Isak Dinesen—Karen Blixen: The Work and the Life.* Translated by William Mishler. New York: St. Martin's Press, 1988.

Johannaesson, Eric O. *The World of Isak Dinesen.* Seattle: University of Washington Press, 1961.

Langbaum, Robert. *Isak Dinesen's Art: The Gayety of Vision.* Chicago: The University of Chicago Press, 1975.

Lasson, Frans and Clara Svendsen, eds. *The Life and Destiny of Isak Dinesen.* Chicago: The University of Chicago Press, 1970.

Luce, William. *Lucifer's Child.* Auburn, California: Audio Partners, 1993.

Migel, Parmenia. *Tania: A Biography and Memoir of Isak Dinesen.* New York: McGraw-Hill, 1987.

Moss, Joyce and George Wilson. *Literature and Its Time, Volume 3.* Detroit: Gale, 1997.

Pelensky, Olga A. *Isak Dinensen: The Life and Imagination of a Seducer.* Athens: Ohio University Press, 1991.

Stambaugh, Sara. *The Witch and the Goddess in the Stories of Isak Dinesen.* Ann Arbor, Michigan: U.M.I. Research Press, 1988.

Thurman, Judith. *Isak Dinesen: The Life of a Storyteller.* New York: Picador, 1982.

Websites

The Karen Blixen Museum in Denmark
http://www.isak-dinesen.dk/engelsk/default.html

Karen Blixen-Isak Dinesen Information site
http://www.karenblixen.com/

Karen Blixen-Isak Dinesen site through the University of Nevada
http://www.nevada.edu/~ddelrio/eng243/blixen/index.htm

Index